THERE AIN'T NO SUCH THING AS HELL

Or the Devil, Demons, Sin, Armageddon, the Antichrist, and Other Such Nonsense

Jim Hoffine

Dare Publications
darepublications@gmail.com
Birmingham, AL

There Ain't No Such Thing As Hell
Or the Devil, Demons, Sin, Armageddon, the Antichrist, and Other Such Nonsense

Copyright © 2014 by Jim Hoffine

All rights reserved. Printed in the United States of America. No part of this book may be used or reproduced in any manner whatsoever without written permission except in the case of brief quotations embodied in critical articles and reviews. For permission write to darepublications@gmail.com.

To Brooke and Dalton,

The Two Great Joys of My Life

Acknowledgment

I would like to sincerely thank those who conceded their time in reading early drafts of this book. Without their suggestions, I would've missed many areas of improvement, both on specific matters and overall content. Specifically, I would like to thank Dalton and Brooke Hoffine, my beloved children, who are two of the smartest people I know. In addition, the suggestions of the very capable Jean Marie Campbell (who also did the cover art), Rebel Negley, and Martha Williams have helped me avoid some of the obvious pitfalls in constructing a book of this kind. As Christopher Hitchens frequently used to remark when he finished a debate oratory: "I'm in your debt."

Table of Contents

Introduction 1

Chapter One: Who Believes This Stuff, Anyway? 4

Chapter Two: What Exactly Is This Stuff They Believe? 11

Chapter Three: Why Do They Believe This Stuff? 37

Chapter Four: The Damage Done By This Stuff 45

Chapter Five: What Is The Bible, Really? 61

Chapter Six: What Is The Church, Really? 107

Chapter Seven: Why It's Totally Irrational To Believe This Stuff 120

Chapter Eight: A Better Way 131

Glossary Of Terms 154

For Further Reading 169

Introduction

I was 10 years old, sitting on a hard wooden chair in the basement of our youth building. It was Sunday morning at the United Methodist Church that my family attended, and my fellow Sunday Schoolers were seated in a semi-circle with me as our teacher spoke. "Children," she said, "What I have to say to you today is very important. Maybe the most important thing I'll say all year." We were all leaning forward, riveted to every word she offered. She continued:

"Do you know where good little girls and boys go when they die?" "Heaven," we all blurted out in near unison. "Now, do you know where *bad* little girls and boys go when they die?" This question, however, was met with complete silence. A few of us sort of knew the answer, but we surely didn't want to say it. Not because we were afraid we might be wrong, but because our parents had told us that the very word in question was a bad word. But she continued:

"Hell! That's where bad little girls and boys go!" We all sort of gasped, and she resumed:

"Now where do you children want to go?" "Heaven!!!," we all shouted again in near-perfect unison. "So are you going to be good, obey your parents, and not get into trouble at school??!" "Yes!!!!," we all but screamed at the top of our lungs!

And this was my first real face to face encounter with the idea of Hell. Oh sure, I had heard a few bits and pieces about it previously, but I had never had it put to me in quite so direct a way. Now the air conditioner was evidently on the blink in our little Sunday School room, and it was quite stuffy in there. This did little to facilitate my comfort as the teacher went on to describe Hell as a hot place, full of fire. I thought to myself, "I sure don't want to end up there, cause *this* room is hot enough!"

And thus began my thought relationship with the odious and barbaric concept of eternal damnation. In the decade or so that followed, my familiarity with the concept was refined, and I came to understand the truly horrific nature of this torture chamber of punishment. It was allegedly a sort of "lake" of fire, where human beings bobbed about, their flesh being constantly ravaged by the never-retreating flames.

Gruesome, indeed. And at age 19 I did what I thought was necessary to save myself from this horrendous possible fate. I became "born again," and asked Jesus to forgive my sins and make me a citizen of Heaven. Thus began my altered relationship with the notion of Hell, a relationship that from time to time in subsequent days still caused me great consternation and anxiety, but from which I was eventually able to extract myself.

My main purpose in writing this book is not to advance the scholarly debate about whether or not Christianity is true. Such debates can, and should, get down into the weeds of issues touching on various areas of science, history, philosophy, and literary studies. Most people have neither the time, nor the motivation, to get into such matters in any detail, and there is a much easier way to approach the question of whether Christianity and its many doctrines are true. So my purpose here is rather to offer the reader an easily understandable way of thinking about Christianity, and specifically the more "negative" aspects of it—such as Hell—and thus to enable her or him to draw a conclusion about the potential veracity of the religion in general. It either *is*, or *is not* true, and one's adoption or rejection of it can (and usually does) have profound implications for one's life.

I trust, however, that my arguments are based upon both sound reason and an appreciation of what science tells us about life. I have also seriously studied and contemplated the Bible for the last 40 years—both inside and outside of academia—and my conclusions are based on what I have learned from both science and modern biblical scholarship.

As you will no doubt infer from the title of this book, I am primarily concerned about human suffering caused by the more horrendous dogma that conservative Christianity advances as truth, although one can make the case that the more "positive" parts of that dogma are often equally as damaging. There are stories, for example, of women drowning their children in the bathtub because they wished to send them to Heaven and out of this evil world. But I myself, as a former evangelical Christian, never suffered a great deal of anxiety about the notion of Heaven, though I certainly did about the barbaric notion of Hell (and other related horrors).

No doubt some of my readers will not have had such a negative experience with Christianity, but even if that is the case, I encourage you to read on. The alleged realities of Christianity cannot help but influence one's thinking and behavior in all kinds of ways— often very subtly—so an examination of whether they are illusions or realities should be relevant to all of us.

If my words result in helping one fellow human being liberate himself or herself from the emotionally oppressive aspects of literalist or conservative Christianity, then the years spent thinking about, studying about, and finally liberating myself from this quasi-barbaric religion will have been worth it.

Jim Hoffine
Birmingham, AL
March, 2014

Chapter One
WHO BELIEVES THIS STUFF, ANYWAY?

Evidently, almost everybody does. In America, anyway. Now granted, the odious concepts of an eternal place of punishment after death, invisible evil creatures roaming the earth with ill intent, and a final gargantuan battle in which a deity "makes everything right" by means of global war are not unique to Christianity. But Christianity is the main vehicle for these ideas in the United States, and it is these specific concepts I will address in these pages.

If you listen to certain kinds of media, you'll come away with the notion that America is increasingly becoming more secular (less religious). However, as a number of recent polls indicate, that is clearly *not* the case. Americans have actually become *more* religious than they were in the mid-1990's, as the following polling demonstrates:

In 1997, 72% of Americans believed in the existence of Heaven, but in 2004 81% did.

In 1997, 56% believed in the existence of Hell, while in 2004 70% did.

In 1978, 54% believed in the existence of angels, while in 2004 78% did.

In 1990, 55% believed in the Devil, but in 2004 70% did.[1]

And these numbers have stayed relatively consistent over the past decade, which leads me to conclude that America is every bit as religious as it has been at any time in its short existence.

What studies also show (see the excellent enlightening forum transcript at www.pewforum.org/2013/08/19/event-transcript-religion-trends-in-the-u-s) is that Americans have simultaneously become less interested in organized religion. Fewer people say they attend church, and rather describe themselves as "spiritual, but not religious." What all this means, apparently, is that even while darkening the church doors less frequently, Americans are increasingly believing in the core concepts of Christianity—at least at the moment.

So the question arises, "Has America been duped with a false religious dogma for all of its history, or do all of these things actually exist?" I mean, either these horrendous things are real, or they are not. They can't be both. And I hope that you will follow me through the pages of this book with an open mind, because I can assure you these things are an illusion. They don't exist. They aren't there.

Now the polling results above don't show us any detail about what, for example, people believe in any detail about Hell. They only show us that a majority of Americans believe it exists (7 in 10). But in my own observation over nearly 50 years, I have seen that different people have different takes on the specifics. For example, though almost everybody acknowledges Hell exists, almost no one believes they themselves are in danger of going there. (Actually, less than one-half of one percent of Americans believe they themselves are going there![2]). Hell is always for the other person—-that black sheep of the family, a ruthless boss, a betraying friend, an ex-spouse, a serial killer, Hitler, and so forth. And many people, while acknowledging that it is real, think of it as sort of a metaphorical "woodshed" where God takes people to punish them for being bad. You know, sort of like when your parents may have used a switch or a belt on you when you were bad. They don't really acknowledge the New Testament's (and later theology's) picture of fiery flames roasting the flesh of still-embodied humans, or that after trillions of years it still has no end. These folks seem to have a sort of disconnect about what the biblical picture is versus the "woodshed" concept they imagine.

And I would say that a great many Americans have a mere nominal belief in most of Christianity's doctrines. They'll quickly tell you, "I'm no atheist, I'm a Christian," but when it comes to submission to Jesus' actual teachings (which granted, are quite radical in nature), they have no interest in participating. Being Christian, for them, is almost equivalent to being American. Sort of the "I believe in God, the flag, the Second Amendment, kicking bums off of welfare, and deporting Muslims" view of being a "Christian." Concern for the poor, turning the other cheek, lending without expectation of repayment, visiting the incarcerated, welcoming the stranger, and other of Jesus' commands are of no interest to them. But they do, as the polls above indicate, believe in Hell, the Devil, angels, and Heaven.

Now my own experience with Christianity was much different. After my conversion in my late teens, I believed in the literal and barbaric idea of Hell—the fire, its never-ending nature, the Devil's presence there, and so on. I also believed in the concept of sin, and that I was inherently a great sinner. And for me personally, the doctrine of *Hell* and the doctrine of *sin* were those which caused me the greatest anxiety—anxiety which followed me around for many years. I was an evangelical, a fundamentalist, a true believer. My commitment was real, and it was deep. But permit me to give a summary of my struggle with those two Christian illusions over the larger period of my life.

For many years, both *prior to* my conversion to evangelical Christianity at age 19, and during the early years of my evolution *out of* that belief system (from about ages 35-50), I worried that I might be headed to that very torturous place. Before my conversion, I somehow adopted the view that things like drinking, pre-marital sex, cussing, and lack of church-going might send me to the Devil's fire. Later, during my slow but steady progression out of that same belief system, I often had fears that if I was wrong in my progressive disbelief in all things Christian, then an eternal roasting might await me.

When it comes to damage caused me by the notion of "sin," I would say that my most affected days were those during which I was a Bible-believing, committed, evangelical Christian (ages 19 to about 35). As a healthy, red-blooded young Christian man in college, I wrestled constantly with what my faith described as "lust." I liked girls—how they looked, how they talked, how they walked, etc.—and on a daily basis I experienced great conflict about it. My very natural response to the opposite sex, a response condemned by my faith, was a cause for constant prayer, self-loathing, and mental gymnastics aimed at eradicating it from my very being.

Of course, I was affected by all beliefs that I adopted during my evangelical days—both "positive" and negative. The doctrine of Heaven, for example, had a more positive effect on me, particularly when grappling with the death of loved ones. And when I would get weary with life I would comfort myself with the thought that one day the Pearly Gates would welcome me—and inside waiting were my own personal mansion and streets of gold upon which I would walk. I have come to see, however, that even the more positive doctrines were having negative effects on my relationship with reality, and I will share more about this later on.

Yes, at age 19 my new faith answered all of life's serious questions for me. If I died, I was headed to Heaven—a very happy and joyous place where pain and death no longer held sway. My purpose on earth became evident—to serve God. And life's tragedies, though devastating emotionally, took on a less severe significance. I was mostly a pretty happy camper during my early months in the faith. But with time, and the honest questions about life and faith that subsequently arose, that happiness and contentment were dampened to some extent.

For example, I would often ask the question "What about my Dad," who had died when I was 11 years old, and who never once spoke about any born-again experience in his life? "Was my Dad roasting in utter agony in Hell, unable to speak to me from Satan's dungeon? My Dad!!??

Whom I had loved with all my heart?" It seemed that for every good thought my new faith brought me, another torturous one would arise.

But enough about my own religious journeys. Let's look at what the general religious landscape of America is.

DIVERSITY, NOT UNITY

When people adopt a particular religious belief system, they do so for a variety of reasons. One of those reasons is that their chosen system meets a group of spiritual or psychological needs that they have. And America is nothing, if not a smorgasbord of religious options. There are, in general, two main options when it comes to Christianity—Protestant and Catholic. But within those two broad choices, there are dozens of sub-options.

On the Protestant side, there are both liberal and conservative choices. The more liberal denominations are the United Methodists, the Episcopalians, the United Church of Christ, the Presbyterians, the Lutherans, etc. On the more conservative side, there are the Baptists, the Assemblies of God, the Pentecostals, and of course the Bible-church movement. The Bible churches are not organized into a denomination, but constitute very conservative, evangelical, "Bible-believing" Christians who meet in church services, Bible studies, and loosely-planned events of all kinds. I myself was a Christian of that type.

On the Catholic side, the organization is a little more rigid, because all churches formally answer to, and derive their doctrine from, the Vatican in Rome. But even here, there are dozens of more or less conservative or liberal sub-groups. In fact, in practice a fair number of American Catholics pay little attention to official church doctrine, but nonetheless remain members of the church.

And within all denominations or groups, there are subcategories among the denominations and Bible-churches. There are conservative and liberal Lutheran churches, Presbyterian churches, Baptist churches, etc. Even the evangelical tradition has a fair amount of variation within its ranks (contrast Joel Osteen with John Hagee, for example). And to confound the issue even more, if you quizzed the individual members of any given local church body, you would find some fairly significant differences in belief and practice. For example, in the first church I attended after my conversion we were always arguing about something—e.g., whether incestual rape was grounds for a Christian to have an abortion, the doctrine of "election" (has God already chosen who is to be saved, and no others can participate?), whether dancing and alcohol consumption were sinful, and a host of other things.

But the main point here is that Americans in general are a religious lot, and mostly "Christian" (versus Buddhist, Hindu, Muslim, Taoist, etc.), even though "Christian" means a lot of different things to a lot of different people. This fact—that America self-identifies as Christian— is what is responsible for the dissemination and survival of the doctrines of Hell, the Devil, Demons, Sin, Armageddon, and a bunch of other bogus nonsense you may crossed paths with at one time or another.

I hope all this talk about Hell and roasting family members has not discouraged you from any further reading. Because these doctrines and dogmas are just that—- doctrines and dogmas that were devised by ancient men seeking to peddle their views about God and the world—- and by the last of these pages I think you'll be able to see that you have nothing whatsoever to fear from any of them. Nothing. They were pulled out of thin air by the musings of the ancients, and their survival through many centuries makes them neither worthy of anyone's belief, nor worthy of causing anyone's anxiety or pain.

ENDNOTES

1. These statistics are all taken from Rodney Stark's very excellent analysis of American religious trends entitled *"What Americans Really Believe*: New Findings from the Baylor Surveys of Religion". 2008, Baylor University Press.
2. According to a 2003 study by The Barna Group entitled *"Americans Describe Their Views About Life After Death."*

Chapter Two
WHAT EXACTLY IS THIS STUFF THEY BELIEVE?

Alright, we've seen that a large majority of Americans believe that the things mentioned in the title of this book exist. But what exactly do they believe about the nature of such things? —i.e., the details about them, if you will.

If you ask 100 people that you randomly meet on the street in America what they believe about *Hell*, you're likely to get a variety of responses. Some will say it's "God's woodshed," or "an eternal lake of fire," or "a place where you are separated from God," or any number of similar descriptions. If you ask them how they would define *sin*, you might get a response like "Doing something God doesn't want you to do," or "breaking the Ten Commandments," or "smoking, drinking, and sex outside of marriage," or a variety of other definitions. The same goes for definitions you get about the Devil, demons, Armageddon, and the Antichrist.

But it seems clear that most people who believe in these things have not thought too deeply about them. And who could blame them? They're not topics which inspire happy feelings. But those of us who took our religion very seriously thought *very* deeply about them. After all, if The Devil and his demonic posse were real and were trying to enlist as many people as possible into the ranks of those suffering in Hell, how could we *not* take such matters seriously?

11

The more liberal denominations, and perhaps a great many Americans in general, don't discuss or debate these matters nearly as much as conservative religious types do, but the following is a description of just what the more conservative camps peddle as truth about these concepts. I should mention here that the general themes under discussion here come not so much from the Bible—-as there is constant vagueness and frequent contradiction within its pages—-but more from the various theologies that sprang up after the Bible was collected into its various forms from about 400 CE on. These theologies, and specifically the major ones which originated in the 16th and 17th Centuries CE, inform the doctrinal statements of various church institutions. And these institutions, through their clergy, inform the individual Christian.

HELL

I have already discussed my first encounter with the concept of Hell. It came in a Sunday School classroom when I was 10 years old. But after my conversion to *serious* Christianity at age 19, I began to learn the brutal specifics of this alleged terrible place. Once you died and went there, you were never let out, and it never came to an end. It was *eternal.* You had a body in hell, and you would be burned (but not burned *up*) by real fire. And ten trillion years after you'd been there, the party was only just beginning. Once in, you could never escape.

Think about this for just a moment. Real flames. Burning flesh. Never-ending torment. A pretty gruesome picture, don't you think? To gain some perspective, imagine those unfortunate souls who have experienced being burned here on planet earth—in house or car fires, industrial accidents, home gas line explosions, and the like. Apart from the agony of the event itself, many are left with disfiguring scars, or experience chronic physical and mental problems. And if you've ever burnt yourself on a stove, a lighter, or a campfire, you know the intensity of that pain.

But Christian hell is infinitely worse. You're not released from its fires in a matter of seconds, or even minutes, but continue to be burned for seconds, minutes, hours, days, months, years, decades, centuries, millennia, and millions, billions, trillions, and indeed a never-ending period of time.

So from where did this inhumane and barbaric concept come? Has it always been a part of the consciousness of human civilization? The answer is no, but the evolution of the idea is a complex one. We'll only consider a broad outline of its development here, and the reader can track down the many sources available if he or she wishes to get more detail. [1]

The ancient Near East, and Mesopotamia specifically, is the geographical area from which Christianity ultimately had its origin. The concept of a barbaric, postmortem Hell did not exist in any culture, however, until about 3 centuries or so before Jesus' time. But prior to that time, the ancient Sumerians and Babylonians had a concept of the "underworld"— a place where both humans and gods could enter, and at some point sometimes come out again. It was a dark and murky world, and not generally a pleasant one. But no flames, no eternality, and no torturous pain were present. The ancient Greeks originated the similar concept of "Hades" (and "Hades" was originally the actual name of the god who ruled over the place), but again it was a place where both humans and gods entered and often came out again. (It was not until later Greek myths were conceived and written that the idea of a "two compartment" Hades arose—one for the "good" people and one for the "bad.")

Into this general geographic and philosophical culture the ancient Hebrews sprang up, maybe in the 1200's-1300's BCE, and they adopted a similar view of an underworld begun by the Sumerians and Babylonians. Their name for it, however, was "Sheol," and was the place to which *all* dead peoples went—both the righteous and the unrighteous (cf. Psa. 9:17, 31:17, 49:14; Isa. 5:14 with Gen. 37:35; Job 14:13; Psa. 6:5, 16:10, 88:3; Isa. 38:10).

But again, no flames, no overt pain—just a shadowy, depressing place, where the "shades" (i.e., the dead) dwelled in a "half-existence." Their religious writings, some of which have survived in what Christians call The Old Testament, contained *no* mention of an eternal, flaming chamber of torture. None. Zip. Zilch. Nada.

But the aforementioned Greek idea of a two-compartment Hades influenced the Jews of the 200's BCE and later. It shows up occasionally in the literature of what Christians call the Intertestamental Period (i.e., the period between the writing of the Old and New Testaments. Examples of the two-compartment afterlife can be found in Tobit 13:2; Wisdom of Solomon 17:14; 2 Esdras 4:8, etc.) and clearly forms the basis for the idea of a conscious afterlife where "good" folks are rewarded and "bad" folks are punished. So by this time the seeds of the concept of the hell later advocated by the New Testament authors were planted.

So there was no concept of a hell or an eternal afterlife in the Old Testament. But what does the New Testament have to say about it? This is a complex question, because various New Testament authors had various viewpoints on the subject. For example, Paul seems to believe in an eternal state of bliss (heaven) for the believer who dies, but always pulls up short of calling the unbeliever's fate "eternal" and is not at all clear about whether that fate even involves punishment. Luke, on the other hand, admits that punishment exists for the non-believer after death, but that it is not eternal. Matthew and Mark very clearly state that both Heaven and Hell are eternal.

Alan Bernstein, in his very excellent work *"The Formation of Hell,"*[1] summarizes the evolution of thought from a neutral, or non-moral view of death—i.e., that one's current life in no way affected what happened to him after death—-to the idea that one's behavior in life determined one's fate after death:

"The bifurcation of death occurred in both the Greco-Roman and Jewish cultures, which informed the Christian idea of hell. Though in different ways, ancient Greece and ancient Israel moved from an undifferentiated, morally neutral view of death to one that considered postmortem fates a consequence of how one lived. The biggest difference between them was that the older, Deuteronomic view never yielded ground and is still fundamental to Judaism, whereas the differentiated or moral view was a late and relatively minor current. The differentiated view was crucial to the legend of *1 Enoch* and gained momentum in the intertestamentary period, becoming a powerful force in Jewish life at the time when Christianity arose. By contrast, the neutral conception of death in ancient Greece did not have the staying power it demonstrated in Jewish thought. Philosophical trends gained more ground. Certainly, it was the philosophical strain, particularly in the Neoplatonists of whom Augustine was so fond, that Greek thought most influenced Christian eschatology. Even without philosophy, however, the Greek stamp on Christianity is apparent in the terminology in which its ideas about death are expressed. Gehenna, Hades, and Tartarus are technical terms in the Greek New Testament. Jerusalem may have turned its back on Athens, but it always knew where it was." (pp. 336-337).

The various *theological* doctrines of Hell, however, were developed over the centuries after the writing of the New Testament books. And, like all theologies, they are attempts to take numerous isolated and often contradictory statements from The Bible and arrange them into nice, neat, harmonious categories. But I don't want to get into a detailed discussion here about the massive amount of scholarship about, and theological manifestations of, this very nasty doctrine, cause we'd be here forever! I will confine our discussion to the actual words that, as Professor Bernstein has pointed out, became the formal terms for postmortem punishment in the New Testament. There are three primary words involved: 1) Gehenna (used 11 times), 2) Hades (used 9 times), and 3) Tartaros (used once).

Gehenna is most frequently translated "hell" in modern translations of the New Testament. The Greek word itself is a transliteration of the Hebrew words *"gay-hinnom"* ("The Valley of Hinnom"), which in the earliest days of the Hebrews referred to the valley of Hinnom located at the base of Mt. Zion. It was in this valley that horrendous things went on, including the sacrificing of babies to various Canaanite gods (e.g., 2 Chr. 28:3). In later times the valley was used as a garbage dump, with fires burning all day and night. Not only were the most repugnant kinds of garbage thrown into the place, but the bodies of dead animals and criminals were as well. If a body didn't make it to the bottom of the ravine, and thus perched on the side of the hill leading to the ravine bottom, then maggots would infest it in short order. Hence the reference to "worms" in some of the statements about Gehenna in the New Testament (e.g., "where their worm does not die."). At some even later point the term took on a metaphorical meaning, and was used to refer to the fiery place of punishment for those who rejected the Christian message (nobody ever argued that "hell" was literally located in the Valley of Hinnom; Mk. 9:44-48). Characteristics of it in the New Testament include fire (Matt. 5:22), and the place where the souls and bodies of the wicked are destroyed by God (Matt. 10:28). It can also set the tongues (i.e., the speech) of the living on fire (James 3:6; this apparently means Hell can cause people to say evil things, which corrupts both their bodies and their life).

Hades seems to be similar to the older Greek concept of a place where both righteous and wicked men go after death, perhaps with a separate compartment for each. This seems to be the case in the story of the Rich Man and Lazarus (Lk. 16:19-31), where Lazarus goes to "Paradise" (the pleasant compartment, where there is water to drink) and the rich man goes to a fiery compartment of torture. In the Book of Revelation (20:14), both "death" and "hades" are cast into the "lake of fire" (= "Hell/Gehenna"?), so *Hades* and *Gehenna* are different places in the New Testament. Starting to be confusing, isn't it?

Tartaros is only mentioned in one place in the New Testament, and actually occurs only in the form of a verb ("to cast into Tartaros," 2 Pet. 2:4). It refers to a place where wicked angels were imprisoned until the Day of Judgment, and darkness is prevalent. This verb is translated "cast into hell" by most modern English translations, although in ancient Greek mythology Tartaros and Hades were two separate places.

However, as mentioned above, there are several places in the New Testament where the concept of Hell is mentioned without the actual use of the word. For example, in Matthew 25 it is referred to as a place of eternal fire prepared for the devil and his angels (v. 41). In other places it is referred to as a place where the wicked dead person's "*worm* does not die (i.e., "worm" = the maggots feeding on his flesh), and the fire is never quenched" (Mk. 9:48). The point here is that the punishment is never-ending, as opposed to temporary— as being eaten by maggots in the midst of a fire would normally suggest. The big finale in the Book of Revelation refers to Hell as a "lake of fire," which burns "day and night" with brimstone and sulphur. Into this lake are cast the Beast, the False Prophet, the Devil, Death, Hades, cowards, the faithless, the detestable, murderers, fornicators, sorcerers, idolaters, and liars (Ch. 20).

It is not my purpose here to try and untangle the many obscure and sometimes contradictory meanings that all these New Testament passages exhibit. One need only look at the confused state of Christendom about the issue to see that this obscurity has resulted in many different dogmas about Hell. The conservative Protestants mostly believe that you live, you die, and then immediately at death you go to either Heaven or Hell. The Catholics have a more nuanced doctrine of afterlife punishments, and one that is not entirely clear. It's main difference from the Protestant doctrine is the addition of the intermediate state of *purgatory*, from which one may be redeemed and journey to Heaven.[3] But even Protestants have an increasing split about whether Hell is everlasting.[4] And to my knowledge, the exact location of this awful place is rarely stated with any conviction by any of them.

Suffice it to say that in general, the notion of Hell is one of the most abominable ever conceived by the mind of man, consisting of humans being brutally burned, perhaps feasted upon by maggots, and incarcerated for either a long duration or for eternity. And don't miss the historical reality that this idiotic notion had its birth in the minds of men in the two or three centuries just before Jesus' time. There was no such idea in most of man's existence—it is an idea that popped up just over two thousand years ago. And let me stop again and say at this point, because such discussions are disturbing at the least, that *no such place exists*—and we will get to the proof of that later in these pages.

My Own Experience With Hell

Fear of going to Hell has at times been a stumbling block to my own state of contentment in life, and mostly in two periods of time. The first occurred sometime in my late teens, when I was beginning to reflect on things I had casually heard or been taught about the matter.

During my early teens, I was never too concerned about Hell. I was mostly distracted by the things my peers were interested in—girls and music. But later on I added sex and parties to my behavioral repertoire, and this coincided with a certain evangelical movement which had invaded my school. Certain of my friends in high school became caught up in the Youth for Christ movement, and had spoken to me about the need to be "born again" by accepting Jesus into my heart as my personal Savior. They also told me that most of what I was interested in—sex, parties, and rock music—was sinful and would be my ticket to Hell. I began to develop a sense of guilt about my behavior and posed the question in my mind: "What if the Youth for Christ people are right and I am headed to Hell?" After all, I had done all of these 'sinful' things and did not have the forgiveness for them through Christ.

So one summer night in 1971, smack dab in the middle of the time when the nationwide "Jesus Movement" hit Birmingham, some pretty girls invited me to a home Bible study. I accepted the invitation, mostly because there were pretty girls involved. At that study I was asked to pray the "sinner's prayer," and I did. I was sincere, and for the next few months I attended an evangelical church. However, just before September, a Christian friend asked me if I'd consider going to Bible College. My mother didn't think too much of the idea—-arguing that a Bible education might not play well in the job market—-but I went anyway.

At some point just after the first semester began, my commitment level to Christianity stepped up a notch—I became 100% committed to evangelical Christianity and intent on Christian service as a vocation. The college itself was not affiliated with any denomination, but was very fundamentalist in doctrine and practice. Their essential philosophy was as follows: Christ is the only way to Heaven (and to thus avoid Hell), the Bible is the absolute and inerrant word of God, and "holiness" is the only way to walk close to God. The holiness part for them—apart from the obvious components of praying, reading The Bible, and going to church—-consisted of no smoking, no drinking, no drugs, no sex, short hair for the men, and long dresses for the women. They even went as far as giving out demerits and grounding those who did not keep their dorm rooms clean, or who otherwise went against school policy. I towed the line (most of the time), because I believed in their doctrine and believed they were doing "God's work."

At some point, however, as I studied the Bible and the Greek and Hebrew behind it more deeply, I began to question some of the assumptions in their fundamentalist view of things. I'll elaborate more on this later, but suffice it to say that I began to have doubts about certain minor things. This doubt once in a while also brought on some minor dread about that old concept of Hell I thought I had escaped. I would occasionally ask myself, "Are my doubts originating from the Devil? Am I really saved?"

After graduating from this Bible college twice (B.S., M.A.B.S.), I ended up at the University of Wisconsin in Madison (which is the main campus). My love of Hebrew gained at the Bible college level had motivated me to enroll in Wisconsin's Hebrew Studies program on the graduate level. Three years later, I had earned a Master's degree in Hebrew/Old Testament, and completed the coursework and preliminary exams for the Ph.D. During this time my doubts about the believability of Christianity increased greatly, mostly due to the intense reading and translating of the Bible, archaeological evidences, the study of how the individual books came to be written, and an understanding of how those books were collected and placed into an authoritative canon of "Scripture." My professors at Wisconsin were mostly Jewish, but theology or doctrine was never discussed in the classroom. It was all about Hebrew and other Semitic languages, the literature of the Old Testament and the Near East in general, archaeology, history, and linguistics. The assistant chair of the department was actually an evangelical Christian, but again doctrine or dogma was never discussed in class.

After I left Wisconsin and began working on my doctoral dissertation, I began what I would call my serious stage of deprogramming from the evangelical faith. This occurred over about a fifteen year period, and it was during this time I had some of my worst struggles with the fear of Hell. I was in limbo—I still generally believed in a more liberal view of Christianity, but had logical arguments with myself about whether the whole thing was just an illusion and a fairy tale. At times I would say to myself, "This can't be true....too much evidence against it," and then I'd say to myself "What if I'm wrong, and end up in Hell for eternity?"

At some point around age 50, however, I finally became "dread-free" of the barbarous concept of Hell, when I finally realized once for all that it was merely an illusion, a god-awful notion dreamed up by the ancients, and that the Bible was merely a human invention which had no authority as a window into the supernatural sphere.

So my struggles with the fear of Hell comprised these two main periods—the few years before my "conversion," and the decade and a half during which I was evolving out of the faith. All in all, however, that is a long time to be troubled by something which simply does not exist.

And I know that I'm not the only one who has been damaged by this absurd notion. For example, I have a friend who is a nurse at a mental health facility in Tuscaloosa, AL. She once made the comment to me that "if I could get the idea of Hell and an angry God out of the minds of the residents here, we could empty about half of this hospital." I sometimes wonder if I might have ended up as one of those residents if I had never come to see the truth about this illusory and barbaric nonsense.

So as we look into the matter further in other chapters, I hope you will come to see that there is absolutely no credible evidence that Hell exists, and that the evidence put forth by some segments of Christianity is clearly not believable. To state it in yet another way—it is a false and damnable concept, with a clearly documentable date of origin in the collective thought of the ancients, and no reasonable person should be duped by it. You're not going to Hell, and neither am I. But please read on, and follow me down this very common sense path of reasoning.

SIN

"Sin," like other concepts in Christianity, is almost universally accepted as a reality. Even among non-Christians, or others who culturally identify as Christian but are not particularly religious, the notion of sin is mostly regarded as a given. For most people, it refers to behaving in a way that is contrary to God's express or implied will. In other words, it refers to specific acts (fornication, adultery, stealing, murder, intoxication, lying, etc.) that God has proscribed, or in neglecting to do something assumed to be his will (praying, going to church, reading The Bible, etc.).

But conservative Christianity also adds another dimension—that of "original sin." Original sin is the doctrine that when Adam and Eve (our ultimate parents) sinned in the Garden of Eden (Gen. 3), we ALL sinned, too (Rom. 5:12). Yes, merely being a descendant of this pair makes you a sinner by proxy. Thus all human beings, regardless of their placement in time or of their ethnicity, are sinners. So you get slammed on two fronts: (1) for individual acts of sin, and (2) for being born a sinner. Even if you could somehow live life without committing acts of sin, you'd still be a sinner and deserving of Hell because of your being born "in sin" as a descendant of Adam and Eve. This nonsense forms the basis for such doctrines as the "total depravity" of all humankind (i.e., all human beings are inherently "evil"; first conceived by St. Augustine in the 4th Century CE, and later developed in detail by Reformers like Calvin in the 16th Century), and forms the justification of consigning to Hell babies who die, the mentally retarded, or those who have never heard the Gospel. The usual response (although there are some very minor variations) is that "we ALL should have gone to Hell, so God is shown to be merciful by saving SOME of us."

To such complete inanity I would like to respond with the following few facts. First, there was no Adam and Eve. In order for you to believe that there was such a first human couple, you have to accept that the earth is somewhere between 6 and 10 thousand years old (i.e., the Bible clearly computes the timeline from Adam and Eve to the time of Jesus as spanning about 4,000 years, and we know Jesus lived about 2,000 years ago. So the total age of the earth, according to the Bible, is on the low end about 6,000 years, more likely about 7,000 years, and with some tortuous "logic" about 10,000 years). Science has blown that idiocy out of the water on so many fronts, I don't have the page space to list them all. The earth is actually about 4.5 billion years old, and the evolution of human beings is no longer considered a mere theory—at least by science and those of us who are rational. So "original sin" imparted to us by our first parents Adam and Eve is a doctrine cooked up by theologians who reject science, and who need to try to make a coherent and consistent harmonious theology out of an inconsistent and mythological Bible.

Second, the idea of "sin" requires two assumptions. The first would be that there is a personal, rational God acutely interested in the affairs of humankind on this tiny speck of a planet. The second is that this God laid out (in the Bible, or in the organized church) a list of "don't do's" that humans can in fact "do." If you don't have the first (an immanent God), then there is no sin. If you don't have the second (a legitimate "divine list"), then there is no sin. I don't want to get into detail about these two things at the moment, as we will look at them in more detail later. But for the time being consider that to believe in the Christian idea of sin you must accept the existence of the Hebrew/Christian God "Yahweh," and that He laid out a list of sins in the Bible. That list of sins is long, beginning with disobedience to 613 precepts listed in the Torah (the first five books of the Old Testament), and continuing with mention of specific sins in the New Testament (e.g., murder, fornication, adultery, lust, hatred, drunkenness, lying, envy, pride, lack of mercy, and dozens more).

For some strains of Christianity this has been expanded to include smoking (cigarettes), cursing, smoking pot (or ingesting any drug), dancing, long hair on a man, short hair on (or the wearing of pants by) a woman, uncontrollable laughing, being a political liberal, and many other such a-moral behaviors.

So what are the negative effects that the idea of sin has had on earth's inhabitants? They are numerous, and I'll mention just a few.

First, let's take the example of sexual "sin," or lust. If you are male, and are aroused when you look at a female (unless she's your wife), you have committed a sin (recall President Carter's admission of this sin in the 1970's in an interview with *Playboy* magazine). The same applies if you are a female and look at a male with arousal. (And we can expand that to include homosexual lust as well). Now, lust is either one of two things: It is either a sin as Christians contend, or it is a most natural social and evolutionary response to another human being. As one who rejects the mythology of Christianity, I accept the latter. Lust, or sexual desire for another person, is built into our evolutionary DNA. Lots of detailed studies have been done that show that sexual desire is hard-wired into us—it's one of the most natural of all human responses, and by no means a negative one. Of course, as with other desires, one needs to control it. Many a politician, husband, wife, and young person have gotten into serious trouble by not doing so. The trick comes in keeping yourself from acting on every sexual urge you have. But the inclination or urge itself is as natural as breathing.

The negative effects in conceding that lust is a sin are great. That is, a person will have these very natural feelings occur, but at the same time will believe these very normal feelings are sinful. I can recall, as a student at Bible College, engaging in all-out war with myself on nearly a daily basis. There were pretty girls everywhere, dressed to the nines in most cases, and many were quite voluptuous. As a young man who was very hormonally charged, I was constantly beating myself over the head about the issue. "How could I be such a depraved sinner?" I continually asked myself. This internal battle resulted in great feelings of guilt, and in my being on my knees in prayer quite frequently to request forgiveness. This guilt produced in me a lowering of self-esteem, which was already low due to my belief that all men were depraved and evil to begin with (original sin). I confided this battle to just one or two fellow students who assured me that prayer and keeping my head "in the Word" (i.e., in The Bible) would help me overcome such desire. Overcome such desire??!!! What an abominable and asinine way to view things! I would equate it to feeling guilty about being hungry. Hunger for nutrition and hunger for sex are both as natural as blinking your eyes. But since the Bible said lust was a sin, I bought into it.

Another example of sexual "sin" advocated by many conservative Christians would be the practice of masturbation. Now there is no explicit reference to masturbating in the Bible, and the practice is as old as humanity itself. But since a person normally fantasizes "illicit" sexual experiences when one engages in it, it is deemed to be sinful. So here is yet another example of the highly destructive nature of believing in sin. A great many studies have shown that the build-up of semen in males has both negative psychological and physical consequences. Lack of release of built-up semen creates psychological stress, and has been linked to prostate problems as well. Again, I consulted a couple of my fellow students on the issue, and was told that this is why Paul said that marriage was better than being consumed by lust (1 Cor. 7:9). I guess they meant that I'd better find a wife, quick, whether I was ready for marriage or not. I must also mention a rather creative answer to the problem that was offered by one of the professors at the college. "Just meditate on Scripture while you do it, and you won't be sinning!!" Well, I tried that, and it was akin to trying to self-gratify while sitting waist deep in a tub of ice. It didn't work—a real psychological "buzz kill" if you will. But this is the kind of insanity that such beliefs can foster.

Other examples where belief in sin causes damage in our experience would be in the areas of divorce, drinking alcohol, "cursing," lack of church "tithing," wearing a certain type of clothing, having body piercings, and the like. I am certainly not arguing that divorce or alcohol consumption cannot be bad things when practiced in a wrong way, but they are not *sin*.

So belief in the biblical doctrine of sin often produces guilt in a person, which simultaneously produces low self-esteem. It is one of the most abominable ideas ever to be conjured by man, and it needs to proceed, along with the other idiotic notions under discussion here, to the philosophical garbage heap of ridiculous ideas.

Now some have accused me of rejecting the notion of sin because I want to absolve myself from the responsibility of living a moral life. Or because I want to propound the theory that "anything goes" in the moral sphere. This is nonsense, because it assumes that a code of morality can only originate from Christianity and the Bible. Hundreds of morality codes have been advanced in many different cultures and times, and some to me are better than what we find in Christianity (and by "Christianity," I mean primarily what has evolved into modern Christianity—which is quite different from what Jesus purportedly taught). Some of the most moral people I know are agnostics and atheists, perhaps because for them morality is not rigid obedience to some external code, but a way of behaving that issues from the heart. In other words, they are not compassionate or empathetic because they are trying to avoid some punishment or get some reward—they have instead personally concluded that a moral way of living is the right thing to do. I will return to this topic later on.

But let's be clear. There IS such a thing as bad behavior, or *evil* if you will, and I would argue that it is mostly driven by man's self-interest. Robbery, rape, violence, theft, greed, murder, two-facedness, deceit, etc. can all be traced to the selfish impulse in human beings. But again, the existence of "sin" requires the existence of a specific God who spells out a list of sinful things. I will argue shortly that there is no clear evidence of such a being, and therefore that there is no such divine list.

So reader, be of good cheer! Much of what you've assumed or thought was sin is no such thing. Sin does not exist.

THE DEVIL AND DEMONS

I recently spoke to a neighbor who was describing the day she moved into her condo. In one room, the former tenants had scribbled all kinds of bizarre symbols on the wall. The symbols were unfamiliar to her, but her comment was interesting: "You could just feel the presence of Satan in that room. When we first saw those scribblings, we immediately knelt down and prayed that God would cleanse and sanctify the place." She, of course, is a devoted evangelical Christian. But her belief in this evil being is even quite common among nominal believers and non-Christians.

Closely associated with belief in the Devil is belief in demons. Demons, according to most of conservative Christianity, are evil spirits who can motivate people to do "anti-Christian" things, or who can actually inhabit a person's body. Modern belief in "demon possession" is pointed up by such movies as the 1977 film *The Exorcist*, in which a little girl is possessed and tormented by a demon.

But even the less devout believe in the Devil. He is pretty much a universally accepted character (although he is allegorized by some religious dogma), and one that roams our planet at will. He's always being blamed for this thing or that, either in the personal sphere (as, for example, in the words of 70's comedian Flip Wilson's old "Geraldine" character—"The Devil made me do it!"—or in the political sphere, where Satan has been said to be behind liberal legislation or the theory of evolution[5]). So we must ask: Are Satan and demons real beings, who function in our society in concrete ways, or not?

The Bible, as usual, is not a unified or clear textbook on the subject. In the Old Testament, despite some unfortunate translations of the Hebrew word *ha-satan* as "Satan" (Job 1:12), there seems to be none of the modern view of an evil being who is intimately involved with the human race. The reference to "Satan" in Job chap. 1 seems to indicate a member of the heavenly court, perhaps an angel or other such being, who acts as a sort of prosecutor. This advocate tells God that Job is only righteous because he has all the blessings of earthly existence—wealth, family, etc. "Take that away," he says, and "Job will no longer be loyal to you, but will in fact curse you."(Job 1:9-11) Proof that no special being is indicated here is borne out by use of the definite article ("the") here—which is not used with names. He is "the accuser," (from the Hebrew verb root *stn*, "to accuse") not the "Satan" of later evolved religious thought.

The reference to "Satan" in 1 Chronicles 1 is ambiguous, however. Here it is said that he (Satan) stood up against Israel and caused David to number the people in a census. There is no definite article in the Hebrew text, so this may be a proper noun (a name), indicating that by the very late composition date of the book of Chronicles (400-250 BCE) there may have been a notion of a specific supernatural adversary working against God's purposes. (Of course there is a further problem here, because 2 Sam. 24:1 says that "Yahweh" motivated David to number the people of Israel; more on that later). But since the Hebrew word *satan* often refers to human adversaries in the Old Testament (e.g., 1 Sam. 29:4; 1 Ki. 5:4), such a meaning may be the writer's intent here.

By the time of Jesus, however, Satan (identified as "The Devil" in Rev. 20:2)—as a definite supernatural being who opposes God—is fully developed. He has a kingdom here on earth (Matt. 12:26), he possesses people (Mk. 1:21ff.), he tempts Jesus in the wilderness (Matt. 4:1ff.), he is a murderer and a liar (John 8:44ff., where the Jewish religious elite are said to act in accordance with their father the Devil), he masquerades as an angel of light (2 Cor. 11:14), he's like a lion looking for people to devour (1 Pet. 5:8), and is a defeated enemy in the coming cosmic struggle portrayed in the Book of Revelation (chap. 20).

He is never physically described in any biblical writing, and most of the horns, pitchfork, tail, red color, etc. are later inventions of imaginative artists and authors.

Likewise, the idea of demons is not present in the Old Testament (passages like Isa. 34:14, Lev. 16:10, 1 Sam. 16:14 are best not understood that way), but very pronounced in the New. Demons cause illnesses or chronic conditions by inhabiting people (Lk. 11:14, etc.), are oddly familiar with who Jesus is (Mk. 1:24), are said to be "unclean" (Lk. 9:42), can be "cast out" of people and inhabit swine (Matt. 8:28-34), and have Satan as their leader (Matt. 25:41; 2 Pet. 2:4).

So as with much of Christian dogma, these ideas of supernatural evil beings are not found in the Old Testament, and are later philosophic or religious concepts developed during the Intertestamental period and thus current at the time the New Testament authors penned their works in the 1st and 2nd Centuries CE. And it is important for our discussion that the reader see that many of the concepts included in the title of this book had a definite, historical point of origin that can be pinpointed. These ideas were cooked up by the ancients, mostly between about 400 and 100 BCE, and have not always existed in human culture.

My Own Experience with The Devil and Demons

It was not until my evangelical conversion at age 19 that I took the idea of Satan and demons very seriously. But I had rubbed shoulders with those concepts before that. My first recollection of being scared about the Devil was related to an episode of Rod Serling's TV show *The Twilight Zone* that I saw when I was 8 years old. The story revolved around a man who had been incarcerated by a group of monks who thought he was the devil. He convinced a visitor to the monastery that the monks were crazy for thinking this, and begged this poor man to remove the "Staff of Truth" that secured the lock on his jail door. The visitor eventually does so, the man emerges, and as he walks across the floor he is slowly transformed into the clichéd vision of Satan—with horns, a cape, pointy ears, etc. This scared the hell out of me at the time (I was young!!), and I guess psychologically it sort of convinced me that such a being could, and probably did, exist.

But the fine points about devils and demons would not cross my sphere of consciousness until much later. Once I had attended an evangelical church, and later an evangelical Bible college, this cacophony of nonsense was front and center in my thinking. Now, certain behaviors or natural urges that I experienced could be blamed on somebody else: the Devil, who "made me do it."

But most of what affected me negatively about the idea of Satan and demons could be found in a couple of my later experiences—the occasional night when I dreamed of Satan or some demons chasing me, and waking up to feel an "eerie" presence in the room. And the annoying and twisted notion that maybe Satan was deceiving me into thinking I was really saved, when in fact I wasn't. This kind of toxic dogma is some of the most damnable in all of Christianity, and I suspect that there are many others who have similar agonizing experiences. At any rate, reader, fear not—because it's all an illusion. There ain't no Satan, there ain't no demons, and we will soon get to why that is a fact.

ARMAGEDDON

The idea that there is a coming final, global battle, when God and his righteous forces will defeat the Devil and his evil ones, is shared by many of the world's religions. In Christianity, and especially conservative Christianity, it refers to that final battle when God defeats Satan, and secures eternal peace for his people (described in some detail in the Book of Revelation). Evangelicals sometimes disagree about exactly when on the final Divine timeline this cataclysmic end will come (e.g., some say before the 1,000 year millennium of peace, some say after), but they all agree that it is coming—and *soon*.

In recent times we have seen various dates claimed for this final end of the world. Y2K (January 1, 2000) was one such predicted date, May 21, 2011 was another,[6] and Dec. 21, 2012 was yet another.[7] While Christians don't generally accept any specific date (citing Jesus' words that "no one knows the exact day or time"; Mk. 13:32), they almost all agree that the date is near. "We're living in the end times" is an oft-repeated phrase both in Christendom and in polite society generally.

In support of their claim that the end times are upon us, they cite various Biblical "prophecies" about the rebirth of the nation of Israel in

1948 (Mk. 13:28-31), the perceived increase in the number of earthquakes of recent times (Matt. 24:7), the perceived notion that America is becoming increasingly "godless," and other perceived notions of strange meteorological phenomena—"Signs in the sun, and moon, and stars" (Lk. 21:25).

Expectations of the end of the world have existed in Judeo-Christian culture from the 1st Century CE—-when the Gnostics[8] believed that God would judge the world in a final battle during their lifetime—-to the present. Indeed, even Jesus allegedly said that some living in his day would witness it (Matt. 16:28). But in each generation the end never comes, and it is left to the next generation to fashion new doom and gloom scenarios for their time.

The ways in which this gloomy frame of mind is harmful to us are usually somewhat subtle. Very few are acting upon it in rash ways, such as selling all their possessions and living the high life for a few months, or dropping out of society to lead a prayerful secluded life. Some do, but the harm with most people is usually more subtle and progressive. Some simply have a generally underlying pessimism in their overall daily outlook on life. "We're in the end times," or "last days," they think. But even worse, some people have actually let their fear of the impending end of the world determine their overall calendar for life—they work less hard, focus less on a successful plan for retirement, or plan less for keeping their families financially afloat in case of the premature death of the family's breadwinners. There are also cases of people living in fear, stocking up food supplies or purchasing extra weapons, or even building underground bunkers to avoid the conflict. In the US this religious perspective sometimes overlaps with those who are ideologically "survivalists"— that recently growing group of people who fear that the federal government will soon declare Martial Law and start incarcerating people.[9]

But there is an equally harmful effect that this "end-time thinking" can have on our society as a whole, and it has to do with its effect on how some politicians formulate policy. I have no inside knowledge of this on the national level, but given the number of conservative politicians who believe this nonsense, I suspect it affects their judgment when they contemplate things like going to war. I have often wondered what was in the mind of George W. Bush when he made the decision to invade Iraq in 2003. As one analyst noted:

"Unlike most other presidents, George W. Bush does not separate his faith from politics. Bush sees 'politics as a religious vocation, a calling, and a sacred duty to be performed for God and humankind.' Bush has stated that he prays that he be as good a 'messenger of His will as possible.' For personal strength, Bush consults not his father, the former president of the United States, but the heavenly Father (Berggren 616)."[10]

Did Bush subconsciously (or consciously) believe that the United States had an apocalyptic role to play in the balance of power in world?—i.e., the idea that "We're the righteous nation with the holy mission of conquering an evil nation that is part of the confederacy of countries that will move at Armageddon against Israel in the last days." Who knows for sure? But plenty of other voices have seen in world events a "God versus evil" drama unfolding, which will culminate in that final battle of all battles—Armageddon (Rev. 16:14).

It would be worth mentioning here another way in which belief in the very near collapse of our world affects our actual world—i.e., opinions about Climate Change. Science has established that our planet is warming, and that the man-made emission of carbons is causing it. This is not under serious debate by the scientific community. It's a fact. However, a great many who bear the moniker "Christian" believe that—even if man-made global warming is true—it's not much cause for concern, because God is about to end the world anyway at Armageddon. This causes them to ignore calls for carbon-emission restrictions, or to vote for politicians who are climate-deniers. (To be fair, however, there is a small but growing segment of evangelicals who are advocating for environmental issues, including the restriction of carbon emissions).

But the point here is that there is no coming Armageddon. No final apocalyptic battle in which God physically intervenes and crushes all evil men and nations. No Rapture (1 Thess. 4:17), no Tribulation (Rev. 2:22, 7:14), no thousand-year millennium with Jesus at the helm (Rev. 20:4-6), or any such nonsense. We are only in the "last days" as humankind if we *want* to be, or *allow* ourselves to be. If mankind cannot find a pragmatic way to coexist on this planet, then perhaps we *will* destroy ourselves, and human evolution will have to start over. But there is zero evidence that any divine "end times" scenario exists, and in the following pages you will see why.

THE ANTICHRIST

Closely related to the fallacy of Armageddon and the last days is a figure who is popularly referred to as "The Antichrist." The term is a New Testament one, and refers to some person—either a contemporary of the New Testament author, or one who was yet to exist in the future. In this person the Devil is said to either incarnate himself or to possess him. He is thought to be part of the "end times" scenario, and specifically is the one who will head up the anti-God coalition that will be defeated at Armageddon (Rev. 19:17ff).

Like most biblical concepts, the actual biblical literature on the subject is vague, but theologians beginning with Irenaeus in the 2nd Century CE have sought to create a neat, harmonious theology around him. The word "anti-Christ" occurs 4 times in the New Testament, all in 1 John, but several other New Testament terms and descriptions have been linked to him by those who create systematic theologies on the subject. Some theologians connect him to the "man of sin" mentioned in 2 Thessalonians 2:3. This person will set himself up in the Jewish temple, claim divine authority, and work false miracles and signs.

Some connect him to the "little horn" of Daniel 7 (cf. also 11:36-37), the "abomination that causes desolation" in Matt. 24:15, and the Dragon, Beast, False Prophet, and Whore of Babylon mentioned in the book of Revelation.

When it comes to identifying this "Antichrist" with a particular person of history, however, the list has been long. Ever since the time of the church father Irenaeus (early 2nd century CE), who suggested that this person might be Jewish by nationality, speculation has been rampant throughout Christendom. The Protestant Reformers identified various Popes as The Antichrist, and the fervor to identify him has only grown more pronounced since The Reformation. Here is a partial list of many historical persons who have been tagged with the moniker:

Antiochus Epiphanies, the Roman Emperor Nero, The Pope (in many centuries), the emperor Charlemagne, Napoleon, Aleister Crowley, Franklin Delano Roosevelt, Benito Mussolini, Adolph Hitler, Joseph Stalin, Francisco Franco, John F. Kennedy, Henry Kissinger, Spanish king Juan Carlos, the Ayatollah Khomeini, Ronald Reagan (yes, for real—-after all, he had 6 letters in each of his names!: "Ronald Wilson Reagan"), Mikhail Gorbachev, Sun Myung Moon, Yassir Arafat, Louis Farrakhan, Bill Clinton, Bill Gates, Prince Charles, Jacques Chirac, and of course in our day Barack Obama. The rule of thumb seems to be, "If there is a powerful person that is your political or religious foe, then he must be the Anti-Christ."

That such identifications are nonsense is based on two facts: 1) there is no coming anti-Christ, and 2) even if there were, the "Scriptures" don't speak with enough clarity about this figure to make any exact identification possible.

But can you see the devastating impact that belief in this myth can have? I personally heard two separate individuals say during the 2008 presidential election that it was "very likely" that Barack Obama was the Antichrist, based on the sheer popularity and fervor that he generated amongst his admirers. The "end times" mentality that is prevalent in this country has a significant number of our populace speculating that some current political figure may be the "man of sin," and this could easily lead to anarchic or homicidal behavior. After all, if you thought that a political candidate or public official was possibly the great agent of Satan, you would not only *not* vote for that person, but would likely go about spouting this nonsense to other Americans, who could easily get whipped into a fervor to "do something about it." And given the spate of violence that we've recently seen inside our borders, it seems clear to me that enough crazies already exist to answer a call to assassinate a public figure.

But fret not, oh reader, cause we are about to wade into the waters of common sense and evidence-based thinking, where fairy tales are not allowed, and notions of metaphysical realities that have no basis in reality will be debunked. It is a liberating place, where ghosts, goblins, satans, burning fire pits, end-time anxieties, and antichrists cease to have free reign over your mind and emotions.

ENDNOTES

1. In addition to online encyclopedias and Bible Dictionaries or works of Theology, see the following: Alan E. Bernstein, *"The Formation of Hell*: Death and Retribution in the Ancient and Early Christian Worlds." Cornell University Press, 1993; Alice K. Turner, *"The History of Hell."* Harcourt and Brace, 1993; for conservative Christian views see *"Hell on Trial*: The Case for Eternal Punishment." P&R Publishing, 1995; Christopher W. Morgan & Robert A. Peterson, *"Hell Under Fire."* Zondervan, 2004.
2. Bernstein, *op. cit.*, pp. 205-247.

3. The doctrine of *purgatory*, or the idea of an intermediate, purging state between death and heaven, was officially developed by the Catholics in the First Council of Lyon (1245), Second Council of Lyon (1274), the Council of Florence (1438–1445), and the Council of Trent (1545–63).
4. See Morgan & Peterson, *op. cit.*
5. Paul Broun, Republican congressional representative from Georgia, recently said this on 9/27/12: "All that stuff I was taught about evolution and embryology and Big Bang theory, all that is lies straight from the pit of hell. And it's lies to try to keep me and all the folks who are taught that from understanding that they need a savior."
6. Harold Camping, the leader of an independent Christian ministry called "Family Radio Worldwide" based in Oakland, Ca, came up with this gem.
7. This was the infamous "Mayan Calendar" debacle.
8. The Gnostics were one of the 3 largest organized groups of Christians living just after the time of Jesus. They, along with the Ebionites, were declared to be heretics by the "proto-orthodox" group in later centuries, and they and their writings mostly ceased to exist.
9. For a representative group who peddles this idiocy, see "The DC Clothesline" (http://dcclothesline.wordpress.com)
10. http://www.studentpulse.com/articles/266/6/the-bush-presidency-undermining-the-separation-between-church-and-state

Chapter Three
WHY DO THEY BELIEVE THIS STUFF?

No *credible* person, as far as I know, has ever actually claimed to have *seen* Hell, the Devil, Demons, the Anti-Christ, or for that matter Heaven, Angels, Jesus, or God. And yet hundreds of millions of earth's human inhabitants, both past and present, have believed that they exist. And believed it with conviction, sometimes to the point of willingly suffering death and great personal loss because of that belief. Why is this?

If we consider the general question, "Why do people become religious?," there are many answers—e.g., to find a sense of purpose and order in an otherwise seemingly purposeless world; to assuage feelings of guilt or fear; to find comfort in the midst of tragedy; or just to have a venue in which to socialize (church/temple/mosque, study groups, etc.).

But in this context I want to focus on the question, "Why do people become religiously *Christian*?" It's a fact that no baby exits the womb with any religious perspective whatsoever, so *why do a majority of us in America end up self-identifying as Christian?*

There are many answers to this question, but I'd like to focus on what I consider to be the three best answers. And they are not mutually exclusive in most cases:

1. Because we were born here, as opposed to somewhere else in the world.
2. Because our parents raised us to believe in a certain Christian tradition.

3. Because we attended a church, or were exposed to some other Christian influence, which seemed to provide something we needed emotionally and psychologically.

BECAUSE WE WERE BORN HERE

Imagine, if you will, that you had been born in the city of Riyadh, Saudi Arabia. As you began to grow and perceive this new world around you, you became able to receive messages from all kinds of sources. If your parents were devout Muslims, they would begin to teach you about Allah, his prophet Muhammad, and the Koran—Islam's main holy book. As you reached school age, perhaps you attended a school that also taught Islamic doctrine. And perhaps your schoolmates, also tutored by their parents in that tradition, became a *de facto* support group for your beliefs. Imagine then, as you became older, you began to hear that Islam is an exclusive religion—that is, the only *true* religion. All other religions—including Christianity, Hinduism, Judaism, and Buddhism or Confucianism (the latter two of which are not actually religions in the strict sense)—were false. You naturally believed that to be so, and could anyone blame you for having this point of view? Of course not. It had been drummed into you from an early age, and your culture group reinforced it at every turn.

The same is true for every person raised in a conservative Christian, Jewish, Hindu, or Buddhist home. What you are taught in your formative years sticks with you more often than not.

BECAUSE OUR PARENTS RAISED US IN A SPECIFIC RELIGIOUS TRADITION

After I became converted to evangelical Christianity, I quizzed a number of people about their religious faith (it was what we were supposed to do).

I can't count the number of people who told me "I was raised a Baptist," or "I was raised a Pentecostal," and for that reason they accepted the entire belief system of that particular denomination without skepticism. And why not? If they respected and trusted their parents, who taught them a particular set of beliefs and carried them to church regularly, it is entirely understandable that they would be hesitant to question those beliefs. Or perhaps they were relatively unconcerned about whether *what* they believed corresponded to actual reality—i.e., was *true*. I find that a significant number of people in America never seriously ask the deep questions about religious belief—if it works for them, why question it? They seem uninterested in asking the very important question: "Is what I believe actually true, or an illusion?"

BECAUSE WE FOUND A CERTAIN TYPE OF CHRISTIANITY THAT SEEMS TO HELP US COPE WITH LIFE

I must inject my own experience here, because this is the exact reason why I converted to evangelical Christianity at age 19.

I have always been an inquisitive person, and this was evident from an early age. I remember traveling down a flat Kansas road with my grandfather in his Oldsmobile, at about the age of 7 or 8. He was on his way to pick up some turnips at a neighbor's farm house, and had asked if I wanted to ride along. Immediately I had squealed "yes!," because I loved and idolized my granddad nearly as much as I did my parents. After we had reached our destination, and he had loaded a fair number of turnips into the trunk, I asked him if we could eat one. "Oh no, Bub," he said (he would often lovingly refer to me as "Bub," which seemed to give him a sense of satisfaction), "these turnips need to be cooked before they'll taste good enough to eat!" In my mind I must never have heard the word "turnip" that whole afternoon, because when I saw them being loaded into the trunk I was convinced that they were not turnips, but were instead stalks of *celery*. Now I *loved* celery, and knew that celery was not supposed to be cooked. So as we were riding back home, I asked him again and again if we couldn't just stop and eat one. He must've seen that this might be a teachable moment for me, and finally relented: "OK, but you won't like them. They're turnips, not celery, and they're bitter until they're cooked." "That's OK," I said, still convinced that what was concealed in the trunk was actually celery, and that my grandpa was wrong. So he pulled the car off the road onto the shoulder, followed me around to the back of the car, and popped the trunk. I quickly grabbed a turnip, bit deeply into it, and got the shock of my life. It was awful—bitter, nasty, and certainly NOT celery! He looked down at me, and with all the compassion of a good grandfather, said "See. It's not celery. Let's go home and get you a cold pop to wash the taste out of your mouth."

One would think that I might have learned a great lesson from that experience, but evidently I did not. Because I repeated the same idiotic scenario with my Dad in a New Orleans restaurant not many months later. But that time it involved a wild onion, which again looked for all the world like celery to me. I mean, it was green and cylindrical, just like celery. My dad kept telling me, "Don't eat that, son, it's an onion." But I bit down into it, and the tears flowed.

My point here, however, is that I don't think most Christians have this kind of inquisitiveness. "If it works, don't ask too many questions," seems to be their usual attitude. Now some would argue that my behavior with my Dad and Granddad was more like obstinacy than skepticism, and they would be right. But my inquisitiveness in later years was actually what drew me into Christianity in the first place.

In my late teens I began to ask some serious questions about life. "Why are we here?" "What is the truth about God and the universe?" and "What is the meaning of all the tumult in the world today?" Coupled with some sense of guilt about how I was living my life, I had come to a place where I wanted answers in the worst way. And it was just about this time

(1971) that the "Jesus Movement" hit Birmingham. (The "Jesus Movement" was a nationwide wave of Christian evangelism in the early 1970's that emphasized the conversion experience in a new and "hip" way. It was independent of any denominational affiliation, and you didn't have to cut your hair, or wear a suit, or join a church to "get saved." Some in the media referred to it as "hippie evangelism.") All of a sudden many of my partying friends were abandoning their weekend drinking and drug use, the continual quest for sexual liaisons, the wild road trips and the like. They were settled down, sober, celibate, and talking about how Jesus had transformed their life. I was astounded at this, and wanted to know more. So one evening I agreed to attend a Bible study conducted by a very conservative evangelical woman, and I soon found what I then believed were the answers to life. She said "Jesus died for you, and if you'll accept him as your Savior you'll go to heaven when you die." "Wow," I thought, "this is just what I've been looking for!" So in a very sincere way I believed, said an "acceptance prayer," and walked out of that Bible study believing I had finally found what I was looking for. Additional Bible studies answered further questions I had been asking about life—questions about our purpose here ("to serve God"), how God wanted us to live as Christians ("in holiness" —meaning no booze, drugs, sex, cigarettes, but remaining in constant prayer and Bible study), and what the meaning of all the turmoil in the world was ("fallen, depraved man acting out his sinfulness"). It was *just* what I needed—emotionally, psychologically, and physically.

And I think that most people, whatever faith tradition they adopt, do so for similar reasons. After all, life is indeed tough—loved ones die, personal and professional disappointments visit most of us, and the news media brings us images of horrible things on a regular basis. Marx once said "Religion... ...is the opiate of the masses,"[1] and he was right. It is indeed a highly effective coping mechanism for what is admittedly a very difficult life for most people, and it's no wonder that so many of us adopt some form of it.

Of course, the fact that something is effective at helping us brave the winter portions of life has absolutely nothing to do with *whether it is true or not*. Many people mentally construct inaccurate and untruthful alternative "realities" about life, just to get through it. Christianity is one such construct, and so are the other religions of the world. In some ways I wish I could passively accept religious dogma, because life seemed to be less complicated when I actually did. But in reality, I'm glad I can't, because I don't want to live my life believing in a lie and an illusion.

But I also wonder if it's not the case that many Christians *don't care* if what they believe is actually true, because so many with whom I speak don't seem to have any interest in questioning its origins. They're sort of like the elderly lady who, while driving her old Buick, was asked if she knew what made it go. "Who cares," she replied. "It gets me where I'm going."

We have examined some of the more fundamental reasons why religion, and specifically the Christian religion, has held such sway amongst we who live in the U.S. and in the West in general. But we have not discussed the actual *mechanisms* whereby the Christian religion has come to us over the past 2,000 years. These mechanisms, so to speak, are 1) the Bible and 2) the (historical) Church. I would suggest that the reader think of these mechanisms as *witnesses* in a court case, because they are similar. They burst onto the scene of human history a little less than 2,000 years ago as a pro-active force with a distinct message: "Believe in Jesus Christ!" And hundreds of millions of earth's residents have responded and done just that.

So we must now ask, "Are these witnesses credible?" "Can they be believed?" "Should we trust them?" If we were to answer *yes* to these questions, then there would have been no need for this book, or for the thousands of other similar responses to Christianity that have arisen throughout history. But if these witnesses are found to be *un*credible, and not worthy to be believed by any rational person, then we must reject that message.

If the New Testament documents had never been written, and the earliest followers of Jesus had not established groups of converts that eventually evolved into what we call the Church, there is no telling how the world would look today. Perhaps some other religious figure, such as *Simon Bar Cochba* from the early 2nd Century CE[2] would've inspired a mass following and we would be attending meetings to study the documents about his life and to praise him. No doubt some religion would've arisen to fill the void.

But the New Testament documents *were* written and collected into their current form and number, and the church *was* begun and eventually disseminated world-wide with the great help of the Roman authorities in the 4th Century CE, so here we are.

However, I would suggest to you that the two witnesses upon which Christianity has been brought to us are *not* credible, and thus are not worthy of our belief. In Chapter Five I will begin to explain why, but in the next chapter we'll consider some of the damage done by Christian dogma.

ENDNOTES

1. The full quote was "Religion is the sigh of the oppressed creature, the heart of a heartless world, and the soul of soulless conditions. It is the opium of the people." Karl Marx, *Critique of Hegel's Philosophy of Right* (never published). His point in that essay was that the poor, who have no chance of happiness here on earth because of their low economic status, turn to religion which promises them happiness in the future afterlife. Hence, it functions for them much like an opiate would.

2. Simon Bar Cochba (Simon "Son of the Star"), was a Jewish leader who established an independent Jewish state in the early 130's

CE. In 132 CE he led a revolt against Rome that lasted about 2 years. The revolt was put down by the Roman military and Bar Cochba was killed in 135 CE. Many Jews of that period believed he was the one about whom Numbers 24:17 had spoken: "There shall step forth a star out of Jacob, and a scepter shall rise out of Israel, and shall smite through the corners of Moab." However, after his revolt failed and he was killed, the current Rabbis renamed him "Simon Bar Cozeba" (Simon "Son of Lies," or "Son of Deception."). He was a significant and powerful force, however, and considered to be "Messiah" by a large number of Jews until his death.

Chapter Four
THE DAMAGE DONE BY THIS STUFF

In 2007 the noted journalist and now-deceased Christopher Hitchens released a book entitled "god is not Great: How Religion Poisons Everything."[1] True to his style and his considerable intellect, it is an incredibly engaging read and full of his rational musings about why religion in general is bad. And while I agree with most of what he penned in that volume, I have to say that he went skimpy on the areas in which religion does have its positive effects. For example, if you've ever contemplated the family members of a recently deceased relative standing before the casket, and seen how comforting was their belief that this was not the end of things —that they would indeed see that family member again in Heaven—then you'd have to concede that religion can have its good side. Or again, if you've ever known a drug-addicted person who converted to Christianity and got sober for a longer or shorter stretch of time, then you'd have to see some positive aspects of religious belief.

However, as noted earlier, the fact that something "works" or can have a positive effect on a person has absolutely *nothing* to do with whether or not it is *true*. And Hitchens is quite right about the preponderantly negative effects that Christianity, and especially conservative (or fundamentalist) Christianity has on life in the U.S. or on the world's populace in general. In this chapter, I'd like to discuss a few of these effects, without asserting that the list is all-inclusive.

DAMAGE TO THE INDIVIDUAL

Christianity, mostly in its more conservative forms, negatively intrudes into the life of many of us in various ways.

The Doctrine of Sin.

The notion of "original sin," developed into an elaborate systematic doctrine long after the New Testament writers were gone, is one of the worst ideas ever to originate in the mind of man. It states that every human being, regardless of race, social class, or gender, is born *evil*. This is, they assert, because we are all descendants of Adam and Eve, our primordial first parents, who "fell" into a sinful state when they ate that apple in the Garden of Eden (Gen. 3:1-7). And that "sin nature," as they refer to it, is passed on to every living being born since Cain and Abel. This idea is nowhere found in the Old Testament, but is most clearly stated in Paul's Epistle to the Romans in the New Testament:

"Therefore just as sin came into the world through one man (i.e., Adam; 5:12)… ….so one man's act of righteousness (i.e., Christ's death on the cross for our sins) leads to justification and life for all." (5:18)

And in post New Testament times this notion of original sin was spun into high gear by various theologians. John Calvin (16th Cent. CE) is probably the worst offender, because he most fully developed the doctrine of "total depravity" (in his seminal work, *"Institutes of the Christian Religion"*). Total depravity essentially says that all human beings are not merely *sinful* as Adam's descendants, but are completely corrupt, evil, dark-hearted, and there is not one iota of goodness in them. Of course, for Calvin and others who subscribe to this doctrine, you can behave righteously if you believe in Christ and obediently submit to his leading in life. But, you are STILL totally depraved.

It's all a tidy bit of theological inventiveness—on both Paul's and Calvin's parts— but it is complete nonsense and leads to some of the worst results imaginable. I mean, talk about your *low self-esteem*!!! According to this dogma you are a rotten, depraved, piece of biological garbage that deserves eternal, fiery punishment in Hell's dungeon, and you just "lucked up" by God sending his Son to die for your abominable nature and behavior. I have met, and continue to meet, many conservative Christians who think of themselves as trash, and that they were merely divinely scooped out of the filthy landfill of moral depravity and sin. "I'm saved," they say, "but I'm still a fallen and depraved person deserving of eternal damnation." And this, I submit, is sad. Very sad.

Of course, there are some conservative Christians who adopt an opposite view of themselves. They de-emphasize the "depraved" part and conceive of themselves as morally superior and of greater worth than the rest of humankind. And you get all kinds of self-imaging views somewhere in between.

Closely tied to the notion of original sin (and our inherited "sin nature") is the notion of individual, real-time acts of sin. The list of sins is long, and each infraction is not always derived by Christian communities from the biblical writings. But in the New Testament biblical list, we encounter such sins as *fornication, impurity, licentiousness, idolatry, sorcery, enmities, strife, jealousy, anger, quarrels, dissensions, factions, envy, drunkenness, carousing, wickedness, evil, covetousness, malice, murder, strife, deceit, craftiness, gossiping, slander, God-hating, insolence, haughtiness, boasting, calling your brother a "fool," rebellion against parents, faithlessness, heartlessness, ruthlessness, sodomy, slave-trading, lying, perjury, stealing, bearing false witness, greed, obscene talk, silly talk, vulgar talk, avarice, pride, folly, and gay/lesbian sex* (Gal. 5:19-21; Rom. 1:26-32; 1 Tim. 1:9-10; Rev. 21:8; Matt. 5:22, 28, 32; 19:18-19; Eph. 5:3-7; Mk. 7:21-22).

I won't even get into the Old Testament list, which is even more extensive, and intensely barbaric—e.g., children's disobedience to their parents, for which they are to be executed (Deut. 21:18-21).

Add to this list the "sins" enumerated by some Christian groups (based on questionable interpretations of some of these words and statutes), which include dancing, singing, women wearing pants or having tattoos, men having long hair/earrings/tattoos, oral/anal sex (in or outside of marriage), masturbation, alcohol in any form or measure, smoking (cigarettes or drugs), wearing skimpy bathing suits, etc.

The Catholics have a more organized view of sinful behavior, and have traditionally divided sinning into the lesser or "venial" sins, and the more serious "mortal" sins (see the *Catholic Encyclopedia*).

Now most rational persons would consider many of these behaviors to be bad behaviors (e.g., jealousy, greed, slander, lying, etc.) and some governments have even passed laws against a few of them (e.g., murder, perjury, etc.). Almost nobody would argue that these behaviors aren't wrong, bad, evil, or whatever one might wish to label them. And such an evaluation comes from an innate sense of what seems self-serving, inequitable, or otherwise improper in a civilized world. But they are not, as discussed before, *sin*. Remember, the commission of a *sin* requires the existence of a specific god who has compiled a list of "don't do's", and a human being who has "done" something mentioned in the list. The Hebrew/Christian god does not exist, so he has not written a "book" containing a sin-list, no deity is thus offended, and therefore nothing can rightly be deemed to be *sin*. (As I've said several times now, we WILL get to the proof of that).

And let me add another anecdotal illustration of the kind of damage this kind of thinking about sin can accomplish. After I graduated from Bible College, and before I went to graduate school, I worked as a house and apartment painter. One of the members of my church had a paint contracting business, and he asked me to come to work for him. As we were painting an apartment interior one day, he was chatting about how he and his wife had spanked their newborn baby the night before. "You spanked your baby?," I asked, knowing that the infant was only a few weeks old. "Yes we did," he confidently replied. I asked him why, and this is what he said: "The baby was crying, and stretching out his hand, and we don't allow that in our house. All human beings are born in sin, and from the get-go they are selfish and sinful. If you don't begin discipline from the very start of a baby's life, then you'll have lots more trouble out of them later on!" I was slightly stunned, knowing that babies often cry because they're hungry, thirsty, crave a parent's touch, or are tired or sick. Not because they are "sinful." I didn't really say much back to him, since he was sort of my boss and I didn't want to seem intrusive, but boy would I like to have that moment back. "You spanked your baby because he was crying?" I would say to him today. "You need psychological help." I don't know how that child turned out, but if his father was beating him at the age of 3-4 weeks, I imagine he received much worse treatment from him as he grew older over the years. I would be surprised if he turned out with a positive sense of himself, or with the capacity to be content with his life. And I wouldn't be surprised if he then went on to inflict pain on his own children. That most children need some kind of discipline during their formative years is obvious, but beating a baby is barbaric and beyond the pale. And the doctrine of sin, in this case "original sin," was the catalyst here. It still angers me to think about it.

And furthermore the convergence of certain natural desires that some human beings have and the list of "no-no's" in the Bible causes great grief to many people. Take, for example, the notion that homosexuality is a sin. In recent times, plenty of scientific evidence suggests that a person's sexual orientation is determined at birth. Therefore, if you are gay, in most cases it's because you're hard-wired genetically or biologically to be so. Just like heterosexual persons are hard-wired to be hetero. Just like you are hard-wired ethnically to be white, black, brown or otherwise. Or to be a blond, a brunette, or a red-head. Or have blue, brown, or green eyes. There is no "sin" involved whatsoever.

Or take the example of heterosexual desire. If you are sexually attracted to a member of the opposite sex, it's because evolution has programmed that into you. And it is not "unnatural" or "sinful." You can repress the desire, and some people do, but it is still part of your genetic heritage. Of course, like any aspect of life, use of this very natural desire is best conducted with common sense and personal responsibility. You can't have unprotected sex with a multitude of partners without risk of contracting an STD, or engendering a pregnancy that is unplanned, or perhaps complicating your emotional life. But sexual activity of any kind—homosexual, heterosexual, married or unmarried—is not *sin*.

The Doctrine of Hell.

You would be hard pressed, I think, to find a more reprehensible, disgusting, barbaric, or ugly concept than the conservative Christian notion of a never-ending fiery torture chamber reserved for those who don't accept the exclusive doctrine of believing in Christ. The particulars of this concept have already been discussed, as have some of the cultural effects (Chapter Two). But a few more are in order here.

Let me start with how this concept occasionally plagued my own Mother. My Mother, may she rest in peace, was a saint. And by saint I mean that she was one of the most selfless, non-manipulative, giving human beings I have ever known. She was a devout Christian, but not in an offensive way. She related to *every* person in the same way—with acceptance. It didn't matter if they were rich or poor, black or white, American or not. She treated everybody the same. And she didn't have a manipulative bone in her body—-she never sat around trying to figure out how to "get over" on others in order to rig life's game in her favor. She was also the most transparent person I have ever known. If you did something that bothered her, she would say so, but always with an eagerness to hear your side of the story. I don't think I've ever met anyone, past or present, who did not have the deepest affection for her. She faithfully attended church, read her Bible and her devotionals, and *always* told the truth.

But she said something one day which has remained with me until the present. Although she believed in the divinity of Christ, and spoke of her born-again experience as a reality, she once uttered these words: "I hope God accepts me into Heaven— because I know I'm a sinner." It was an off the cuff, incidental, buried-in-the-conversation utterance, and I suspect no one but me picked up on it. She believed in a fiery, eternal Hell, and the overwhelming nature of that image affected even her. And based on my knowledge of how she thought, I'm certain that the barbaric nature of this abominable doctrine is what caused even her to question if she were among the forgiven few. I remember thinking at the time, "Wow, if YOU don't make it, then I don't have a snowball's chance."

And she was not the only one with such insecurities. In my evangelical days I ran into countless fellow Christians who faced such chronic anxieties about their spiritual state. Over time I saw hundreds of people respond to the altar call for salvation, even though they had done the very same thing on many previous occasions. They believed, and sincerely so, but the potential horror of Hell still plagued them.

I have even encountered "non-believers" who somehow still feared the flames of Hades. A fellow musician, who had often declared himself an atheist, once told me in all sincerity that he was "probably going to Hell" for divorcing his wife. I said to him, "There's no such place," and he cut a glance at me as if to say "you sure about that?" The cognitive dissonance in his statement was evident to me, but obviously not to him.

The concept of Hell is deeply rooted in our culture, and is so universally accepted that it ranks right up there with acceptance that George Washington was our first President. And even though surveys indicate that 70% of all Americans believe in Hell but less than ½ of 1% think they themselves are going there, I suspect that fear of Hell is more widespread than these surveys indicate. I base that suspicion on my queries of hundreds of people I have known over the course of about 5 decades. It doesn't surprise me that people formally surveyed would respond in the negative when asked "do you believe YOU are going to Hell?" because the same occurs, for example, when you ask people if they are racist. Almost nobody answers that question with "Why yes I am," but if you are a careful observer of our current culture you know that to be patently untrue. There is a significant segment of American society that is racist to one degree or another, and the number is much greater than ½ of 1%.

I have already disclosed my own personal struggle with this awful *meme* that Christianity has injected into our culture, and I'm certain that I'm not alone in that experience. But fear not, reader. There is no such thing as Hell, and you'll see why shortly.

The Devil and Demons.

In 1973, Warner Brothers released the movie "The Exorcist," and a serious uptick of interest in the Devil and demons occurred.[2] Of course, belief in the Devil/demons had been around since the country's founding, but that movie helped to bring it to the forefront of the public's consciousness in a way previously unknown. The phenomenal production values of that film helped produce a picture of what it might actually look like if a human being was possessed by a demon or Satan. Linda Blair also did a phenomenal acting job, the special effects were staggering (for the time), and I was not able to eat pea soup for a long time thereafter. I was a new convert to evangelical Christianity, so I certainly believed that the Devil and demons existed. But this helped me put a "face" on the horror of demon possession. "That's pretty much how it really looks," I said to myself, and for months afterward I dreamed about such devilish things.

The idea that in post-modern 2013 a large contingent of people would still believe in the Devil, his demon partners, and frankly any such thing is astonishing to me. But we *do*, and in large numbers. I'm not aware of any *credible* accounts of anyone actually seeing these beings, but they are routinely believed to be operating behind the scenes of what is visible. Exorcisms are practiced among both conservative Protestant and Catholic church members and clergy, and there are a number of documentaries which chronicle these bizarre proceedings (e.g., *The Exorcist in the 21st Century*, by Akselsen). And the damage caused by exorcisms, or concurrently by a person's belief that she/he is possessed by a demonic spirit, is significant and very pitiable. The poor "demoniac," or person who believes he or she is possessed, has obviously come to believe that something negative in their life has been caused by a demonic invasion of their physical body. That negative thing could be "lustful" thoughts, or chronic anger, suicidal musings, or any number of things that are the common lot of man. But instead of attributing these to natural causes, and subsequently trying to resolve them in rational or medical ways, these poor folks fall victim to something they've been taught by Christian culture, and thus seek out an "exorcist." If you have ever seen one of these rituals, it is bizarre in the extreme. The afflicted person is often in a state of quasi-consciousness, and the exorcist begins praying or commanding the supposed spirit to exit the body of the possessed. There can be laying on of hands, use of "holy water" or a wooden/metal cross, or group chanting. At some point the exorcist makes a final dramatic pitch for the spirit to come out, and the deed is done. There are no phantasms that visibly float out of the possessed's body—- you just have to have faith that they did, and that those evil spirits were defeated by the mighty power of God.

Many of these poor souls sincerely believe that they have been delivered, and return to their everyday lives expecting the best. But when the anger, or lust, or what-have-you returns, they often again believe that they have been possessed. Re-possessed, as it were. Being possessed is sort of the sense that you have "cooties," as we used to say in junior high school, but on a much grander scale. Cooties on steroids, if you will.

Why we continue to give credence to such idiocy is beyond me, particularly since science has dispelled the notion that evil spirits are rampant on our planet. And medical science in particular has identified mental illness as just that, and not the habitation of a human being by an evil spirit. This notion—of equating physical sickness or mental illness with demon possession—was alive and well in Jesus' day (e.g., Matt. 8:16; 9:32-33). Common sicknesses, such as epilepsy, were attributed to those devils, when in fact no such thing was true.

So take heart, reader. There ain't no Satan, no devil, no demons, no evil spirits, and you can live your life free of such irrational fears. I will offer the proof shortly.

Armageddon.

If you ask 100 evangelical Christians if we are "in the end times," 77 of them will say yes. If you ask 100 Americans in general the same question, 41 will say yes.[2] *Armageddon*, or *The Apocalypse* as it is sometimes called, is believed to be that last battle towards which all human history is moving. That final battle when Jesus will appear in the sky and smite his enemies on the earth, thus ushering in the Kingdom of God.

The history of charlatans who have duped the local populace by declaring a date certain for this cataclysmic event is long, and stretches back to the days of Jesus. Jesus himself allegedly believed that the ushering in of the Kingdom of God upon the earth was just around the corner, and said so (Mark 9:1, etc.). But in recent times we've had a spate of end-time hucksters. Harold Camping, the *"Left Behind"* book series, and most evangelical preachers are examples. Of course, the "final day" always comes—and goes—and those who blindly believe such nonsense are left holding the bag. I think particularly about one poor slob who sold all that he had and gave the money away, certain that after May 21, 2011 he would have no need of it. Others have become disillusioned, and suffer confused anxiety when the anticipated date comes and goes—without anything happening.

But the notion that the last days are upon us has far deeper sociological and psychological consequences than just giving your money away. It permeates the psyche of millions of Americans, and casts a dark pall over their perception of life. In the back of their minds they harbor this concept, and when they see the world getting progressively more complicated and volatile they "connect the dots," and think that we must definitely be in the last days. This can have all kinds of real-time effects—-like a generally pessimistic view of life, a fearful view of life, or the sense that very little is worth working or planning for. It can become, for many, a real "buzz kill" for life.

But let me assure you, the general quality of life in the US is vastly better than what it has been for the rest of the world since the beginning of civilization. Up until about 50 short years ago, the world really *was* volatile. History, since the inception of walking Homo sapiens, has been a picture of tribes and nations vying for supremacy in the world. If you were an ancient Hebrew, about every century or two you could expect a warring superpower to come and kill or enslave you, or carry you off as captives to their homeland (e.g., as did the Assyrians, Babylonians, and Romans). If you lived in medieval Europe, about every century or two you could expect neighboring countries or world empires to invade and subjugate you. This more or less was the rule of thumb for all nations until about 75 years ago, when weapons technology (and specifically nuclear technology) began to make the "musical chairs" nature of global shifts of power much less prevalent. Nuclear (and other weapons) technology has been a deterrent to super nations who become lustful for massive expansion. For example, Russia or China, both of whom are significant power players in the world, would presently never consider an invasion of the United States, because the odds of success are nil. We have nukes, bio/chemicals, and a sophisticated military that would make such a move an absurdity. Perhaps the last time we might have had to worry about such a thing occurred just a half century ago, during the cold war in 1963, when we came within an eyelash of nuclear confrontation with Russia. This happened during the U.S. naval blockade of Cuba.[3] But in general the advancement of weapons technology, the birth of global economic interdependence, and (one would hope) the adoption of general common sense make the possibility of "World War 3" an extremely unlikely occurrence.

I should also again mention one other way that "end time" thinking harms us, and it concerns care for the environment. Certain segments of the Christian Church believe that Jesus will return to earth and rapture the church out of it sometime very soon, followed by the complete destruction of the planet by God. So they reason, "Why should we worry about global warming or taking excessive care of the environment? God is going to end history very soon anyway, so it really doesn't matter." This is not only ridiculous, but such thinking will cause massive catastrophe in the long run—disease, loss of coast lines, destruction of large parts of the environment, huge losses of global wealth, loss of animal life, and much more. So believing that "the end" is just around the corner not only is destructive to one's personal felicity and success, it has destructive global consequences as well.

But take heart, reader. There is no coming Armageddon, no biblical Apocalypse. However, one thing that could end us here on earth is religious or political/religious ideology. Some extremist fringes of religion may well make an attempt to execute global mass homicide, and if they get ahold of weapons of mass destruction they may well be successful to a smaller or larger degree. But it will not result in global annihilation. And it won't happen any time soon, if at all.

Armageddon is a religious myth cooked up in the minds of men about two thousand years ago, and you'll soon see why.

The Antichrist.

The *man of sin*, or the *antichrist*—according to Christian theology—is a coming world leader who will dupe the masses and dominate the world political scene. He is either Satan himself, or is a human being indwelt by Satan according to this dogma. I have already discussed the biblical references to him, as well as the failed identifications of him throughout history (Chapter Two), but the damage caused by this nonsense is still being felt in our culture today. I am astonished at how deeply this meme is built into our society, and not just among the overtly religious. Once in a while I hear the following, and always from an extreme political conservative: "I think Barack Obama is the anti-Christ, because he has millions of people swooning over him, and he's always talking about 'peace, peace'." The sheer idiocy of these kinds of comments always amuses me, because if popularity and a desire for peace are the identifying marks of the antichrist, then literally hundreds of world politicians and altruists fit the bill.

And why do these kinds of people think that some *U.S.* politician or philanthropist will be the one? Because here in America many people think *Amerocentrically,* as if the U.S. is ground zero for all meaningful history—and divine history at that. Evidently many Americans didn't get the memo that about 95 out of every 100 human beings on the planet are not American, and our country is in its infancy relative to the rest of the world. Europe, from whence we came, is over two *millennia* old. We are only a little over two *centuries* old. But the notion persists that some *American* must be the antichrist.

So, in summary, this "we're in the last times" thinking damages our political culture, stirs up unfounded hate and fear, and makes people act in inordinately irrational and harmful ways.

But fear not, reader. There is no such person as *the Antichrist,* and we'll shortly see why.

OTHER KINDS OF DAMAGE.

There are many other kinds of damage that belief in these concepts cause to individual persons, but I would like to speak about some of the ways in which it affects larger segments of both our domestic and the worldwide populace. These mostly are related to the world of politics.

In the lead up to the Iraq war, President Bush was asked if he had consulted his father about whether invading Iraq was a wise move. He responded:

"You know he is the wrong father to appeal to in terms of strength. There is a higher father that I appeal to." (Washington Post, 7/4/04).

In other words, reasoning with knowledgeable fellow human beings was only of secondary importance to him. God was the ultimate source that he sought to make that policy decision.

And Professor Bruce Lincoln of the University of Chicago Divinity School concluded this:

"[For Bush] the U.S. is the new Israel as God's most favoured nation, and those responsible for the state of America in the world also enjoy special favour......Foremost among the signs of grace--if I read him correctly--are the cardinal American virtues of courage, on the one hand, and compassion, on the other......Wherever the U.S. happens to advance something that he can call 'freedom,' he thinks he's serving God's will, and he proclaims he's serving God's will."[4]

In short, one can conclude that for certain politicians—found mostly among the conservative ranks in this country—Christian religious ideology that sees America as the ultimate moral arbiter for the rest of the world is foundational to how they formulate policy and initiate legislation. Did Bush conceive of our attack on Iraq, and a potential repeat of that scenario in Iran, as part of the end time calendar of events "prophesied" in the Bible? I can't say for sure—because I'm not privy to the inside of his mind—but his statements certainly seem to indicate so.

For him it was always "good vs. evil"— i.e., America vs. the "Axis of Evil" (Iraq, Iran, and North Korea), rather than America vs. nations who for him posed a threat to our interests or security.

And our current political environment is replete with Republicans who base their policy positions on supposed notions of "sin." Those who cast their Congressional votes against gay marriage legislation are always quoting the Bible as grounds for their positions, and those who seek to decrease funding for higher education bemoan the "secular humanism" of our universities. Add to that those who sit on local school boards and wish to either remove the teaching of evolution from our high schools, or teach "creationism" (read: Bible myths about the beginning of the world about 6-8 thousand years ago) alongside, and you begin to get the picture.

One U.S. Congressman—Rep. Paul Broun of Georgia, who is also an M.D. — even recently said this:

"God's word is true. I've come to understand that. All that stuff I was taught about evolution and embryology and the big bang theory, all that is lies straight from the pit of Hell. It's lies to try to keep me and all the folks who were taught that from understanding that they need a savior."[5]

So you can bet that he will not be disposed to fund public education, which (at least at present) is still primarily teaching science in the classroom.

So you see, from these few examples, that belief in these mythological Christian doctrines has repercussions that go far beyond the individual or our domestic population, but in fact affect millions of people worldwide. Tens of thousands of dead Iraqi civilians could attest to that fact if they were here, and thousands of dead American soldiers could as well. Not to mention tens of thousands of LGBT people who endure social ostracization, abject hatred, lack of job opportunities, and a general lack of the same rights as other Americans have.

Yes, Christian dogma affects millions in various negative ways, but beginning with the next chapter we will see why belief in it is completely unfounded, and why we should begin as a country to retire it to the garbage heap of primitive and disproven mythology.

ENDNOTES

1. Published by Hachette Book Group, 2007.
2. The Barna Group, Summer 2013 OmniPoll.
3. This occurred when we attempted, by dropping practice-grade depth charges, to get a Soviet nuclear submarine to surface in international waters near Cuba. The submarine's captain, not knowing if nuclear war had broken out topside, ordered that a torpedo armed with a nuclear warhead be launched at one of our ships. But Vasili Arkhipov, an officer on the boat and of equal rank with the captain, was successful in stopping the launch. Had it been launched, you and I might not be here.
4. In an interview with *The Village Voice*.
5. See endnote 5 in Chapter 2.

Chapter Five
WHAT IS THE BIBLE, REALLY?

If you asked the average American what she or he thinks the Bible is, you'd get a variety of answers. Answers like "The Word of God," "God's message to mankind," "A Holy Book," or "Divine Stories to Live By." The strict Christian conservatives have defined it as "the inerrant Word of God,"[1] by which they mean that every last word in it is true and without error as it relates both to the metaphysical and to historical events recorded in it. That is, God really did create the universe in six days, the earth is about six to eight thousand years old, there really was a global flood about four thousand years ago, the Hebrews actually did escape in a mass exodus from Egypt, God parted the Red Sea for Moses and stopped the sun so Joshua could complete his annihilation of Jericho's inhabitants, Jesus really was resurrected from the dead and will again visit earth, etc., etc. Less conservative Christians will argue that the message is Divine, but the record of historical events need not necessarily be accurate.

And if you ask the average Christian *where* the Bible came from, some will say that it magically floated down from heaven, bound in a leather cover, with gold-edged paper— in English. More schooled Christians may know something about its human authors, its original form in Hebrew and Greek (actually Hebrew, *Aramaic*, and Greek), but most will never have taken the time to research its evolution from sacred writings composed by the ancient Hebrews (Old Testament), to the combination of those writings with the various writings penned in the century after Jesus' death (New Testament). And almost none will have any knowledge of how those writings were physically transmitted from generation to generation over about a 2500 year time span, to get to the nice, neat "Bible" that they carry around today (transmission of the writings). Add to this a general dearth of knowledge about how each "book" of the Bible got chosen to be in it (canonization[2]), while dozens of other competing books were rejected, and you have the actual state of biblical knowledge amongst Americans today. *Not much is actually known.*

And why bother? It is a cultural assumption that The Bible is something holy, and few are willing or motivated enough to challenge that assumption. It is ingrained in our social self-identification, and generally accepted as readily as the daily appearance of the sun, or the human need for food and water.

Furthermore, few Christians have actually *read* it. Oh sure, most will have favorite one-liner verses from this book or that, learned from church or bible study or an internet posting. But not many have plowed through the rest of "God's Word"—say, for example, the Prophet Micah, or all 66 chapters of Isaiah, or The Epistle to Philemon, or Leviticus, etc. And who can blame them? The biblical writings are culturally much different from our own, the writing style of much of them is tedious, specific historic and cultural references in them are hard to understand, and the total number of pages before the reader is almost endless. In English printed Bibles, there are often about 1500 pages, about the amount contained in 6 or 7 average- length modern books.

But this seems somewhat odd to me. Conservative Christians—those who readily accept the existence of the concepts mentioned on the cover of this book, and who declare with great conviction that "The Bible is The Word of God!!!"—don't know much about it and haven't read most of it. I mean, if you're going to go about claiming that "the eternal and omnipotent God has written a book!," wouldn't you want to scour every page to see what he has said? But I would wager that more Americans have read every page of *"Fifty Shades of Gray"* [3] than have read every page of the Bible. I think comedian Bill Maher had it right when he said that the average Christian relates to the Bible much like they do to the "terms and conditions" boxes that pop up on computer programs—they check "I accept the terms" at the end, without ever having actually read them.

So we must now ask, "What, really, is the Bible?" It is way beyond the scope of this book to give a comprehensive and highly detailed answer to this question, and that has been done in dozens of other places by very competent specialists in the various fields of study, but I offer you this summary:

THE HISTORY OF THE HEBREWS AND CHRISTIANS.

The Bible is primarily a product of Hebrew authors and institutions, so to understand its origins one must understand the origin of both the ancient Hebrews, and that group of Jews and non-Jews who later came to be known as "Christians."

There is some uncertainty about where the ancient Hebrews actually came from—i.e., whether they were a distinct group of people who invaded that tiny stretch of land we currently know as Israel, or whether they may have evolved from within the peoples who were living in that tiny land known at the time as "Canaan." In other words, they may have been a distinct ethnic group who took over Canaan from the outside, or they may have been Canaanites themselves who separated and formed their own national identity. Biblical scholarship at present favors the latter explanation.

We do know, however, the following:

Somewhere around 1000 BCE the Hebrews were able to establish a kingdom. A very small kingdom, indeed, in the context of the established world of the time. It was about the size of Rhode Island, and was situated at the eastern end of the Mediterranean Sea, pretty much where modern Israel is located today. This kingdom was much smaller and less significant in the world than many of its neighbors—the Egyptians, the Assyrians, the Babylonians, etc. —but its philosophical legacy has lasted much longer than many of those nations around them. Contrary to these Hebrews' own claims (in the Old Testament), however, they were never a serious political or military force in the ancient world.

This kingdom consisted of all twelve Hebrew tribes of Israel and lasted until 922 BCE (around 80 years or so), and then it broke apart into two separate nations—-called *Israel* in the north (10 tribes), and *Judah* in the south (2 tribes). However, in 722 BCE the Assyrians from the east came and carried most of Israel into captivity. And, as often happened in those times, exile into a foreign nation spelled the end of those peoples as a distinct national entity. These are the "ten lost tribes of Israel" that you may have heard about. No doubt the Israelites mixed culturally and intermarried with the Assyrians, and over time "Israel" just ceased to exist as a distinct ethnic population.

More than a century later, a similar thing happened to the kingdom of Judah in the south. In 597 BCE, the Babylonians came and carried off the elite population of Judeans. About ten years later this was followed by a more complete exiling of the rest of the Judeans, and we have a sense of what this meant to those exiles expressed in the words of a Psalm: "By the rivers of Babylon we sat and wept, when we remembered Zion (= Jerusalem, the capital of Judah. Psa. 137:1). However, unlike what happened to the northern kingdom Israel, these exiles managed to maintain their national consciousness, and eventually emerged around 538 BCE to return to their homeland and reestablish their nation and temple. If they had not, there would've been no Old or New Testaments as we know them today. Nor any Christianity, for that matter. And much of the Old Testament (or "The Hebrew Bible," as Jews currently refer to it) originated from the rational struggle which the ancient Judeans had coming to grips with how their God could let them be treated with such hostility by their enemies. In short, they were conquered and exiled (in their minds) because of their sin and rebellion against their God. The fortunes of the Judeans (who later came to be known as "Jews") did not fare so well after their return and rebuilding of the Temple which the Babylonians had destroyed, but at least they were able to stay in their homeland—albeit under the domination of first the Medes and Persians (ca. 539-331 BCE), then the Greeks (ca.331-146 BCE), and finally the Romans (146 BCE through the destruction of Jerusalem in 70 CE).

It was in the time of Roman domination that Christianity was born. Jesus of Nazareth—around whom Christianity sprang up—lived from around 6 BCE to about 30 CE. A small band of his followers, all Jews, began to spread stories and messages about him, first throughout all of Judah (roughly equivalent to the geographical position of the southern part of modern Israel—i.e., the southern West Bank and northern Negev desert), then throughout much of the Mediterranean lands both to the north and west. They were greatly aided by new and ambitious followers, namely Paul of Tarsus (= the Apostle Paul) and his companions. During the 2nd Century CE, certain various forms of this new teaching had emerged and become distinct in the Mediterranean area in general, and though the earliest "Christians" (as they became labeled; Acts 11:26) were not organized into a coherent group and did not have a unified message, historical events were about to change that.

In or around 312 CE, the Roman Emperor Constantine claimed to have a Christian spiritual conversion of sorts, and boom! — nearly 70 years later (380 CE under Emperor Theodosius) Christianity was declared to be the official state religion of the Roman Empire. The result of this policy change by the Empire cannot be overemphasized. The competing sects of Christianity were reviewed in councils called by Constantine, and an official form of the new religion was singled out. All other forms (such as Gnosticism and Ebionite teaching) were declared to be "heretical," and were forbidden to be practiced. The considerable amount of literature supporting these "heretical" sects was also declared to be taboo, and the majority of these documents were destroyed. Archaeology in the modern era has uncovered a few of these writings (e.g., the Gnostic *Gospel of Thomas*, *Gospel of Peter*, etc.), but most remain lost at present.

The history of the Christian church, from the time of Constantine until the present, is complex and it is not within the scope of this book to address it here.[4] It is a somewhat bizarre and brutal history, with internal squabbles leading to opposition groups being murdered, tortured, and ostracized. It is also a history of the church intertwining with the state, wherein one influenced the other to varying degrees. But it is worth noting that by the 16th Century a major schism occurred within the institutional church, leading to the Protestant Reformation. The best-known figure of this time was Martin Luther, a Catholic scholar who became disgruntled with the church, and led a revolt that broke from the mother church and established the form of Christianity that is the origin of all "Protestant" denominations and movements in existence today. Conservative American Protestant Christianity, a focus of this book, owes its very existence to the life and work of Luther, who declared that "Scripture alone"—not the interpretation of Scripture by the Catholic hierarchy— was to be the basis for all church doctrine and practice. Luther was not what we'd call an "evangelical" Christian in the modern sense—he still retained many Catholic ideals—but his reformation was game changing in a huge way.

Christianity, of course, came to our American shores with the early western European settlers in the 17th Century, and in various forms— Protestant, Catholic, and with sub-species of the two. The current state of Christianity in the U.S. is a fragmented one, with all kinds of local emphases and distinctions, so that *it is not possible to speak of Christianity as a unified thing*. The only commonality that all sects of the religion have today is use of the name "Christ."

THE OLD TESTAMENT

The "Old Testament," as Christians refer to it (Judaism naturally refers to it as "The Hebrew Bible," since Jews do not consider the New Testament to be Scripture), is a collection of "books" which originated from the ancient Hebrews, who occupied what is generally the geography of modern day Israel. This new tribe of Hebrews, from about 1200 BCE to about 168 BCE, produced a number of stories, histories, law codes, homilies, songs, and miscellaneous material which was ultimately written down and kept by the professional class of scholars, priests, and scribes who controlled the temple worship. The actual books collected and regarded as "holy" over the centuries by the Hebrews were divided into three classes—-The Law (Genesis through Deuteronomy), The Prophets (Joshua--Malachi), and the Writings (Psalms--Chronicles). In modern-day Bibles used by Christians, this arrangement is not followed, and the 24 individual books are further divided into 39 individual books. The book of Daniel was the last book included in the "Scriptures" acknowledged by the Hebrews to be "holy," and it was written sometime around 168 BCE. There were other books written after that, some of which are acknowledged by either the Catholic or Eastern Orthodox Churches as having some divine authority, but the Jews regard the "Minor Prophets" (Hosea-Malachi) as the last of their Scriptures.

THE NEW TESTAMENT

The New Testament as it exists today—which began with the writings of a former Pharisee and scholar named Paul (formerly "Saul" of Tarsus; Acts 9:11)—began to be written and distributed sometime around 50 CE, and ends with The Book of Revelation, written somewhere around 95 CE or possibly later. The earliest Christians were Jews who continued to observe the "Law" of Old Testament Judaism and to attend synagogues, but also subscribed to the new "Way" (Acts 9:2; 19:9, etc.) based on the teachings of the One they regarded as the long-awaited Jewish Messiah—Jesus of Nazareth. Somewhere around 80 to 90 CE, the establishment Jews kicked these new "troublemakers" out of the synagogue, and from that point on they began to organize and become a truly independent group (or actually "groups"). The actual New Testament writings were slowly collected and circulated in various times and places in both Israel and Asia Minor. Since most early Christians were not able to read or write, they depended on going to "church meetings" (usually in someone's house) to hear these documents read aloud. The first church decisions that declared the 27-book collection we have today as authoritative (i.e., that listed them as "holy" or "inspired") did not occur until more than 200 years after this very early Christian period. We will discuss that process in slightly more detail later.

These short summaries are concise in the extreme, but again, it's not my purpose here to engage in a detailed history class about the Bible's origins, but rather to acquaint the reader with some very basic background for the ensuing discussion. Check the sources in the endnotes if you wish to educate yourself about it in more detail.

HOW DID THE BIBLE GET PUT TOGETHER?

Today we can go to almost any bookstore and purchase a beautiful leather-bound Bible, complete with parchment-like pages having golden edges. But this is a very recent phenomenon. For the first 1500 years of the Bible's existence, no such printed copies were available. It is only since the actual invention of the printing press (about 1440 CE) that such a thing has been possible. And in fact it is only within the last century or two that printed Bibles were available to the average person in English-speaking parts of the world.

So let's answer three questions here:

1) How did the specific books that are in the Bible actually come to be written?
2) How did those books get to be chosen as deserving to be included in it?
3) How did the individual books get transmitted before the invention of the printing press?

As far as the Old Testament (Hebrew Bible) goes, the following *very* general summary explains its origins, canonization, and transmission:

1) Origins – The Old Testament

The Torah—the first five books—is comprised of Genesis through Deuteronomy (called "The Torah," meaning "The Law"/"Teaching" by Judaism; "The Pentateuch," meaning "The Five Books" by Christians) and had a complex origin. Modern scholars (since the mid-19th Century) began to notice certain "blocks" of material within the five books that seemed to be unified in outlook, style, and use of God -names. This helped explain why there were doublets, contradictions, and varying viewpoints within the Torah as a whole (e.g., the differences between the Creation story of Gen.1:1—2:3 and the one beginning with 2:4; the differences between certain legal proscriptions, etc.). These "blocks" of material had separate authors and thus separate viewpoints, and were woven into a whole by later editors. This hypothesis was called the "Documentary Hypothesis," and originally identified four main documents—J, E, D, and P. This stood for the "Yahwist" source (J), the "Elohist" source (E), the Deuteronomist source (D), and the Priestly source (P). Each writer (or writers/editors) had a slightly different take on the traditions of ancient Israel, and whoever did the final editing into the Torah we have today *did not go to great lengths to harmonize the differences*. This may have been due to the fact that all the material used by the final editor(s) was considered ancient and therefore sacred, so he (or they) merely wove the material into a somewhat coherent whole without changing the major components of it. And while The Documentary Hypothesis has undergone rigorous scholarly debate (about dates, exact identifications of sources, and viewpoints), the theory is still accepted by the majority of Old Testament scholars today. If you take the time to read the Torah with an open mind, and with this hypothesis before you, it is pretty easy to see that a single author—i.e., Moses according to both ancient Christians and Jews—did not pen all five books. (Or frankly any part of them, for that matter).

The Prophets (as the Jews arranged them), which begin with the Book of Joshua and end with the book of Malachi, had a variety of origins. 1) Joshua through 2 Kings—called the "Former Prophets" by Judaism), are generally regarded as the "history" of Israel as compiled by an editor, or school, sometime after 622 BCE. (i.e., it assumes King Josiah's reforms). Certain references in this collection make it likely that it was composed and edited by some person or persons of the Deuteronomist school (the "D" of J,E,D,P), after the Jews returned from Babylonian exile. 2) Isaiah, Jeremiah, and Ezekiel —standing at the head of the "Latter Prophets" in the arrangement of the Old Testament by Judaism— were collections of the "preachings" or writings of those three Israelite prophets. These would have been compiled at various times and places, and most certainly not all the material attributed to each prophet under his name/book originated with that prophet (e.g., compare the 3 distinct datings and viewpoints contained within the one book of "Isaiah"). 3) Hosea through Malachi—Part of the Latter Prophets but further distinguished as "The Twelve" by Judaism—contain various kinds of material (narrative, speech, etc.) and were composed at various times and in various places by various authors.

(It should be noted that the Catholic tradition adds the books of Tobit, Judith, and 1st and 2nd Maccabees here).

The Writings (as they were called by Judaism) begin with Psalms and end with 1st and 2nd Chronicles. The Psalms were primarily poetic "hymns" sung in the liturgical setting of the second Temple (6th century BCE and later). Proverbs is a collection of wisdom sayings originating over various times and places. Job is a wisdom book of high Hebrew poetry (and probably more ancient than much of the Old Testament), composed by an editor/author using a fairly common motif from the Ancient Near East— the problem of suffering by the righteous. And the rest of this division contains widely differing types of literature, from wedding/love poetry (Song of Songs), to nearly modern existentialist philosophy (Ecclesiastes), to a history re-write (1-2 Chronicles). Special mention might be made of the book of Daniel (the last book of the Old Testament, as Judaism classifies it, written sometime just after 168 BCE), because of its clearly *apocalyptic* nature (beginning with chapter 7). Apocalyptic literature used fantastical images, visions, and dreams, to refer to contemporaneous persons, nations, and events, so as to disguise the author's real meaning (i.e., to keep him out of trouble, as it were, with the political authorities). The book of Revelation in the New Testament is the only other straight up *apocalypse* in the Bible. But the genre was common from about the 2nd century BCE to about the 2nd century CE.

In short, most of the Old Testament "books" were evolved over time and underwent editing, as opposed to being written down by one author at one specific time. And most of that final form "editing" occurred between the 6th and 2nd centuries BCE.

2) Canonization – The Old Testament

That there were more than the current books in the Old Testament circulating in ancient Israel is clear, and even the Bible itself confirms it (e.g., Nu. 21:14; Josh. 10:13, etc.). So with all the written material circulating around, how did the 24 books (= Christian 39) get to be collected into a whole and regarded as "holy?" The question is complex and admits of no easy answer, plus there are gaps in our knowledge of the process. But the following is likely to be generally true.

After the Jews were taken into captivity by the Babylonians (597 BCE and later), the Jewish leaders undoubtedly did not want to suffer the same fate as their brothers in the North (i.e., "Israel"), who virtually disappeared as an ethnic unit through assimilation with the Assyrians. And one way to assure that the distinct national consciousness continued was to make sure the national traditions were both written down and that a specific collection of them was deemed to be "holy." It's a little bit like our writing and declaration of a Constitution and preservation of the Founders' documents here in the US—it provides understanding of our beginnings and what is to be regarded as the laws by which we must live. Of course, the US Constitution is not a religious document (no mention of God in it), there is nothing about "ethnic purity" in it, and it was conceived and encoded in a vastly shorter time than the Old Testament writings.

But sometime during the 400's BCE the Torah reached its final form, while the Prophets reached final status in the 200's BCE, and the Writings not perhaps until the 100's or early 200's CE. The Jewish people lived in different places throughout the Middle East over those roughly 500 years, and different groups made different pronouncements about things, so it is perhaps not terribly helpful to say the canon was "closed" at any specific time or place. But some time by the late 2nd century CE it seems clear that the 24 books of the Hebrew Bible (= the Protestant 39 books of the "Old Testament") were regarded as the final "holy" ones, and the canon was closed.[5]

3) Transmission – The Old Testament

Some of the earliest materials we find in the Old Testament show clear signs of having been transmitted orally (through memorization), which of course is to be expected in a culture in which few people could read or write. And in very early Israel few had the required materials to write, even if they had been able. It would've required a "pen, ink, and paper," as it were. But writing utensils were quite crude and rare in those days, and ink and something to write on were possessed by very few. Those who were attached to the monarchy and to the Temple were the more educated folk, and they were able to write things on "scrolls" made of various materials.

But in our time the earliest full manuscripts of the Old Testament available to us are the ones that were found at Aleppo (920 CE) and in Leningrad (1008 CE). Think of it, there is somewhere between a 700-1900 year gap between when the Old Testament documents were originally "written" and our earliest full copies of them!! What kinds of copying errors or theologically-motivated interjections or alterations may have occurred over that vast amount of time and in the thousands of times they were copied?

But with the discovery of the Dead Sea Scrolls about 65 years ago, we received a general answer to that question. The Scrolls contained many different kinds of documents, but one type were scrolls of the Old Testament books. Most of them were just fragments of the (Hebrew/Aramaic) Old Testament books (excluding the Book of Esther), but the Book of Isaiah was complete. These documents date all the way back to the 200's-100's BCE and show a remarkable similarity to the two codices found in Aleppo and Leningrad more than a thousand years later. There are differences in wording and actual content amount, but the correspondences are remarkable! What we can generally say about the accuracy of the transmission of the Old Testament, at least between about 200 BCE and the present, is that it was very good. Not perfect, but pretty good.

Of course, this has nothing to do with whether the Old Testament was written or inspired by God, but it says a lot about how faithfully the Jews transmitted what to them were their Holy Scriptures, their national charter.

Now concerning the New Testament:

1) Origins- The New Testament

The New Testament is comprised of four Gospels, a history of the Apostles' and others' spread of Christianity (Acts), twenty one "letters" (ostensibly from apostles to various churches or groups of Christians), and The Book of Revelation (an apocalyptic book declaring how the current world would end and the Kingdom of God would eternally take over).

The earliest writings were Paul's (early 50's CE), and the latest was probably Revelation (95-120 CE). The names associated with the Gospels—Matthew, Mark, Luke, and John—were not part of the original documents. The Gospel writers wrote anonymously, and only later in the second century did the church assign names to them. We don't really know who wrote them. We only know that they made the final "cut" (into the current Christian canon) decades after their composition, and the assigning of the names were designed to give them the authority of the persons named (see a full discussion in Ehrman, "*Forged*").[6]

Acts was clearly written by the author of the Gospel assigned the name "Luke," and it describes the spread of Christianity throughout parts of the Roman Empire.

The next section—"The Epistles" ("Letters")—contains mostly personal correspondences between leaders of the church and certain specific churches, or geographical regions that contained churches. The book of Hebrews, however, is a little different in that it addresses no particular group, and is more of an early Christian sermon, and the First Epistle of John is sort of a Christian tractate or dissertation. Paul is claimed by tradition to have written 13 of the Epistles, but most modern scholars believe he is responsible for only 7 of these (Romans, 1 and 2 Corinthians, Galatians, Philippians, 1 Thessalonians, and Philemon).[7] Tradition holds that Peter (the close disciple of Jesus) wrote both First and Second Peter, but modern scholars are nearly unanimous that Second Peter was not written by him. There is considerable modern debate over the authorship of the rest of the New Testament, and it is beyond the scope of our investigation to go into it here.

2) Canonization – The New Testament

That there were dozens (or possibly even hundreds) of other books circulating in the early church is beyond dispute, and a number of them have survived for our perusal. Paul himself refers to other epistles he wrote (but are now lost; 1 Cor. 5:9), and others include The Apostolic Fathers (writings by church fathers in the 2nd century, and considered Scripture by certain Christians), The Nag Hammadi documents (e.g., The Gospel of Thomas, The Gospel of Philip, epistles, apocalypses, etc.), and others still.

And this fact demonstrates that for at least 300 years after Jesus, early Christians were carrying on debates about which books were authoritative—i.e., to be considered "Scripture"—and which were not. This debate was fueled by vastly differing interpretations of Jesus' life and ministry after he had exited the scene. In short, there were the

—- *"proto-orthodox" Christians*—those who eventually won out and whose teachings were accepted as the true Christianity.

—- *Gnostics* —who emphasized a kind of *secret* knowledge that supposedly originated from Jesus. And the

—- *Ebionites* —a Christian group who believed Jesus was the Messiah, but not divine. They also believed that continuing to observe the Old Testament laws and customs was necessary for eternal life. They rejected Paul's letters, and accepted The Epistle of James as central. (see Fig. 1).

But the fact that the "proto-orthodox" community won out and gained sanction by the Roman state is the reason the 27 books in almost all modern Christian canons became "the New Testament." If the Gnostics or Ebionites had dominated the Christian scene of those days, our Christianity and our Bibles would be much, much different. It is worth mentioning here that the first mention of an official closed Christian canon by any notable Christian authority came in 367 CE— by bishop Athanasius of Alexandria, Egypt. This pronouncement came some 250+ years after the last orthodox.

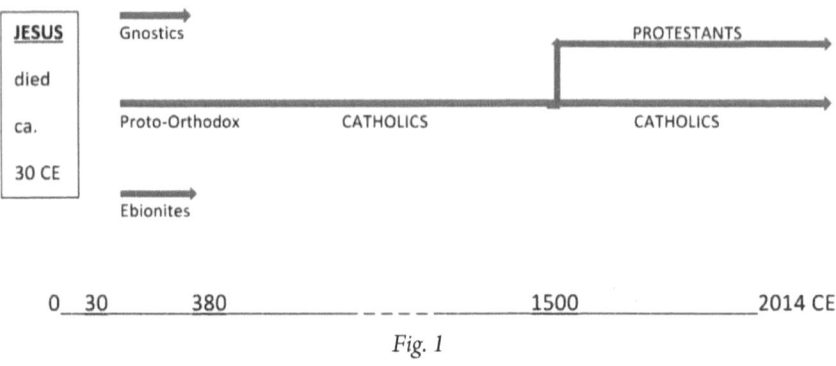

Fig. 1

Notice that after Jesus' death around 30 CE, three main groups of "Christians" emerged in his wake. The Gnostics—who believed that Jesus had imparted a "secret" knowledge to them for distribution to the world; the Ebionites—who believed that Jesus was the prophesied "Messiah" of the Old Testament, but that he was not divine. They also believed that obedience to *the Mosaic Law and belief in Jesus were necessary for salvation; and the Proto-Orthodox group of believers, who developed into the Catholic Church and were declared "orthodox" by the Roman authorities in the 4th Century. If the Romans had opted for either the Gnostics or the Ebionites teaching as the "true" form of the faith, our Christianity today would look quite different.*

Christian book was written (i.e., Revelation), and almost 350 years after Jesus.

In short, it is necessary to realize that Jesus didn't live, teach, and die, and then in the next week orthodox Christian churches appeared on the street corner, in which you could find a copy of The Bible. It took over three centuries—longer than the United States has been in existence—for the early Christians to collectively determine what was "true" (as they saw it), and for the collection of writings we call The Bible today to become a fixture of Western culture.

3) Transmission—The New Testament

The writers of the anthology we call The New Testament did not write their books, take them down to the copyright office, and then Xerox mass copies for distribution to the various groups or persons to whom they were addressed. This is, of course, because neither copying machines nor a copyright office existed at the time. Any writing that was intended for a given audience had to be copied—word by word, paragraph by paragraph—if it was to be transmitted to other places. And of course, in the process of copying, mistakes were made. Some of those mistakes were made simply due to the frailty of the human mind and body, and some were intentional. The intentional ones were made because the copyist didn't like what the particular word or phrase had to say (e.g., it disagreed with some doctrinal opinion of the copyist).

To illustrate, let's say the first person copying a document left out a word or a line, then that omission would be repeated by the second copyist, who might introduce an error or two of his own into the copy. And this was repeated over and over for hundreds of years. The New Testament was copied thousands of times between the time the individual books were penned and the 15th Century CE, when printing presses came into existence and the copying errors essentially ceased. We don't have ANY of the *original manuscripts* of the New Testament, so it's difficult to know the true scope of how much these books were changed after their original authors wrote them. And in fact we don't even have any complete early copies of them—-most of the copies we do have date from several hundreds of years after the originals.

But what we do have is a collection of about 5,000 New Testament manuscripts, and guess what? NO TWO of them are the same in every word. It has been estimated that there are as many as 200,000-400,000 differences in wording amongst those 5,000 manuscripts. That's a lot of differences!! Now, to be fair, most of those differences concern minor things like misspelled words, changes in word order, or accidental omissions of a line. But some concern very major sections of the Bible. Take, for instance, the last 12 verses of the Gospel of Mark (16:9-20). They are not found in any of our earliest manuscripts. Thus, they very likely were later additions by some particular Christian group or scribe. That will no doubt come as a great shock to some who handle snakes or drink poison as part of their church services!! And consider the story of the woman taken in adultery in John 8:1-11—-one of my favorite Bible stories ("He who is without sin, cast the first stone"). It is not in the earliest and best manuscripts, and therefore was almost certainly not a part of the original Gospel of John. There are other fairly significant examples of later additions, but these should suffice to demonstrate the phenomenon.

So how did we arrive at a single Greek text that could be read or translated into English (or any language) for our use? By the science of *textual criticism,* which compares all the various copies, their date, their geographic origins, early quotations of New Testament books by church fathers, etc. The textual criticism of the New Testament is a vast and complex enterprise, done by excessively intelligent and scholarly experts, who then produce for us a single conflated text which we can read or translate into our language. But keep in mind, this conflated text does not match ANY single copy of the roughly 5,000 we possess. It gets us back to some general form of the New Testament that was circulating in the Middle East about 200 years after Jesus.

It has always amused me that conservative Christians came up with the notion that "every word of the Bible is without error, written by God, and true in every sense," when we don't even know exactly what "every word of the Bible" is. Their position on this implies that God was very careful to inspire each and every word of his written revelation, but then became "hands off" when it came to the transmission of that Bible to mankind. That is a leap in logic that I am no longer prepared to take.

This discussion about the Bible's evolution is *very* terse, and intentionally so. I don't want to get bogged down in tedious detail about these issues, but rather want to focus on the form of the Bible we have today. Our consideration of whether it is a *divine,* and therefore *worthy* book to be believed and used by us as foundational for a belief system, has virtually nothing to do with what specific form of it we consider.

Why It's Not Rational To Believe The Bible Is God's Word

I do not think the Bible was "inspired" or ultimately written by any divine being, much less the God of Israel, and I base this on three simple facts:

1) The fact that there are *internal contradictions within the Bible itself.*
2) The fact that The Bible is in *significant conflict with science.*

3) The big picture. The first two reasons just mentioned might be described as "existential" or real-time reasons why I don't believe the Bible is the word of any god. The third—-viewing it in the context of human history and behavior—-looks at the question from a different perspective.

Mankind began walking upright at some point in his evolution, and at some point developed a brain large enough to reason and imagine a being (or beings) greater than himself. Once this occurred, he began to think of his lot on earth as perhaps influenced by things he could not see. In more recent historical times he reasoned that there must be otherworldly causes why certain events—both good and bad for him—-were occurring in his experience. At first, with the appearance of "language," he began to construct stories about gods and demigods. These beings, he thought, were the reasons why the crops grow and he has enough to eat. But these perceived beings were also the reasons why at some times drought and hostile weather conditions killed his crops and he would starve.

In most ancient cultures, stories about their tribal gods circulated orally in the beginning, but when the idea and practice of writing finally evolved, man was able to preserve these stories in a more durable form. Eventually these writings would be gathered into a single collection, so that the "religious" members of the tribe could recount them to the people. The ability to read and write was rare in the ancient world, and only a few possessed the knowledge or the tools to do so.

The Bible is one such collection of "god-stories," if you will, but it is not unique. The Egyptians had their sacred writings (*The Pyramid Texts, The Book of the Dead*, etc.), as did the Babylonians (*Enuma Elish, The Epic of Gilgamesh*, etc.), and the many religious groups which sprang up in the various locales of antiquity did as well. The Buddhists have their Sutras, etc.; the Hindus have their *Bhagavad Gita*, etc.; the Confucians have their *Analects*, etc.; the Taoists have their *Tao Te Ching*, etc.; the Muslims have *The Koran*, etc.; the Zoroastrians have *The Avesta*, and so on. There are literally thousands of such ancient texts. In more modern times the adherents of the Bahia religion have *The Book of Certitude*, etc.; Scientologists have *Dianetics*; and the Latter Day Saints have *The Book of Mormon*, etc. Most of these literary texts have an exclusivist attitude about their teachings, and they can in no way be reconciled to a general viewpoint.

And The Bible is extremely exclusivist as well. The Old Testament is mostly written from the perspective that the Hebrews alone were the chosen people of the one true God (Yahweh), and the New Testament mostly claims that Jesus is Yahweh's son and the *only* way to salvation.

It is in the historical DNA of mankind to formulate religious ideas to explain his world and the alleged world beyond it, and to eventually write these ideas down. The Bible is one such collection of writings, but to assume that it is the one and only repository of truth, and ALL other writings and religions are false, is just not a rational position to take. I submit to you that NO sacred writings, including the Bible, were penned or supervised by a deity, and none of them provide any insight into the supernatural world (if there even is one). This is particularly clear when you consider the first two reasons listed above, and I would now like to expand on them in some detail.

INTERNAL CONTRADICTIONS WITHIN THE BIBLE ITSELF

Let me say by way of introduction that most of the contradictory information found in the Bible has to do with irreconcilable viewpoints about religious matters (e.g., the "wisdom" school versus the Prophets in

Old Testament times, the differing views about the significance of Jesus' life, death, and resurrection by the writers of the New Testament, etc. etc.). But it takes a close study of large amounts of The Bible to be able to see these differences, and most people don't have the motivation to pursue it. However, there are smaller, easy-to-see contradictions within the pages of The Bible and the following is just a small sampling.

The New Testament

I remember the first time I was ever puzzled at something I read in the Bible. I was a student at Bible College, and was merely doing a little devotional reading in my dorm room. I came across this passage, which describes something Jesus said to Peter right after Peter bragged that he would never deny him:

"Truly I tell you, this very night, before the cock crows, you will deny me three times" (Matt. 26:34)

But I had read the account of the same event in the Gospel of Mark at some previous time and it seemed to me there was something different about it. So I turned to the parallel passage in Mark and read:

"Truly I tell you, this day, this very night, before the cock crows twice, you will deny me three times" (Mark 14:30).

So I thought to myself, "What happened here?" Did Peter deny Jesus 3 times and then the cock crowed? Or did Peter deny Jesus once, the cock crowed, he denied Jesus 2 more times, and then the cock crowed again?

To put it in list form, Matthew says:

1) Peter denies Jesus 3 times (26:69-74).
2) The cock crows (26:74).

Mark says:

1) Peter denies Jesus once (14:66-68).
2) The cock crows (14:68)
3) Peter denies Jesus two more times (14:69-71).
4) The cock crows again (14:72).

No big deal, right? So the Gospel writers got some minor historical details wrong about Jesus' life. It doesn't affect the main message of Christianity. Right?

I say WRONG! If you are dealing with people's eternal destinies, mostly based on a book that purports to tell the absolute truth about every detail of Jesus' life, then it IS a big deal. If there is error here, how do we know there is not error in other statements it makes—like what is required to have a right standing before God (salvation), whether there is a Hell and a Heaven, where we go when we die, what is in store for planet earth, etc. etc. etc.!!

Of course, at the time, these passages only puzzled me and did not seriously cause me to question whether the Bible was "the inerrant Word of God," true in all that it speaks about both faith matters and history. But the seed of uneasiness was planted in my mind at that point. As time passed, and I began to get seriously into the study of the Bible, many more questions arose in my mind about similar things.

The following are just a few of the more blatant contradictions found in the Bible, both in the Old and New Testaments.

1) Jesus' death and the Temple Curtain.

In Old Testament Judaism, the section of the Temple called "The Holy of Holies" was thought to be where Israel's God dwelled on earth (Ex. 25-31).

Once a year, on the Day of Atonement, only the high priest could enter that section to make atonement for his sins and the sins of the Hebrew people (Heb. 9:7). What separated this section from the rest of the Temple court was a curtain. In the Gospel of Mark, this curtain is mentioned in the context of Jesus' death on the cross:

"Then Jesus gave a loud cry and breathed his last. And the curtain of the Temple was torn in two, from top to bottom" (15:37-38).

Pretty simple, right? Jesus died. Then the Temple curtain was mysteriously torn in two.

But hold on. The Gospel of Luke has a slightly different time line for the events:

"It was now about noon, and darkness came over the whole land until three in the afternoon, while the sun's light failed; and the curtain in the temple was torn in two. Then Jesus, crying with a loud voice, said, 'Father, into your hands I commend my spirit.' Having said this, he breathed his last" (23:44-46).

The events for Luke have a different time line. While Jesus was still on the cross—*alive*—the temple curtain was torn in two. In other words, Mark says he first died, and then the temple curtain was torn. But Luke says the temple curtain was torn, and *then* he died.

There are reasons the various gospel writers altered the traditions they had to work with, and they have to do with the authors' overall theological perspective and intent. But that is really beyond the scope of our discussion here. On to more contradictions.

2) How Many Donkeys?

When Jesus made his triumphal entry into Jerusalem, just before the events culminating in his crucifixion and burial, he rode down the street on an animal that suggested humble status—a donkey (or a colt). On this point three of the Gospel writers agree. Compare Mark's account:

"Then they brought the colt to Jesus and threw their cloaks on it; and he sat on it" (11:7; it's roughly the same in the parallel accounts in Luke 19:35; John 12:14-15).

But hold on. Rather than riding in on *one* donkey, Matthew has Jesus riding in on *two*:

"They brought the donkey and the colt, and put their cloaks on them, and he sat on them" (21:7).

Now it's easy to see why Matthew changed the story from one donkey to two, because he tells us:

"This took place to fulfill what had been spoken though the prophet, saying, 'Tell the daughter of Zion, Look, your king is coming to you, humble, and mounted on a donkey, and on a colt, the foal of a donkey." (21:4-5)

The prophet he is quoting is Zechariah, whose book probably comes from the 400's BCE (the quoted section, anyway). In one of his oracles, he declares that Israel will have a coming king who will establish his rule globally:

"Rejoice greatly, O daughter Zion!
Shout aloud, O daughter Jerusalem!
Lo, your king comes to you; triumphant and victorious is he,
humble and riding on a donkey,
on a colt, the foal of a donkey." (9:9)

But for some reason, Matthew either didn't understand the concept of *synonymous parallelism* in Hebrew literature, or (more likely) was employing a common type of rabbinic interpretation common in the first century CE, whereby they ignored synonymous parallelism and separately interpreted each of the synonymous phrases.

Synonymous parallelism is found throughout the Old Testament (Amos 5:24; Psa. 19:1), and occurs in Zechariah's verse here twice. It is a literary device in which *one* thought is stated *twice*, with slightly different wording. "Rejoice greatly, O daughter Zion" and "Shout aloud, O daughter Jerusalem" mean essentially the same thing. Similarly, the statements that the king will come to them "riding on a donkey, on a colt, the foal of a donkey" mean the same thing. One animal, not two.

But whatever the reason, Matthew has *two* asses, and the other three gospel writers have *one*.

3) Poor Judas

All the Gospel writers agree that Judas was the one who betrayed Jesus to the Roman authorities. But what happened after that? The agreement vanishes from there. Mark and John don't discuss the matter, but Matthew and Luke (in Acts) do. Matthew tells us that after Judas did his dirty deed, he was upset that Jesus was condemned and took the money he was paid for his betrayal back to the priests:

"He said, 'I have sinned by betraying innocent blood.' But they said, 'What is that to us? See to it yourself.' Throwing down the pieces of silver in the temple, he departed; and he went and hanged himself. But the chief priests, taking the pieces of silver, said, 'It is not lawful to put them into the treasury, since they are blood money.' After conferring together, they used them to buy the potters field as a place to bury foreigners. For this reason that field has been called The Field of Blood to this day." (Matt. 27:4-8)

So, according to Matthew, the priests took the money and bought a field (perhaps a field where potters used to go to collect clay used in making their pottery), where the Jews could bury foreigners who died in their country. And note here that Matthew says this field got its name—"The Field of Blood"—-because the money the priests used to purchase it was "blood money" (i.e., money used to get an innocent man condemned).

Luke, however, has quite a different take on the matter. Quoting part of Peter's speech to about 120 people in Jerusalem after the death of Jesus, he has Peter say:

"'Friends, the scripture had to be fulfilled, which the Holy Spirit through David foretold concerning Judas, who became a guide for those who arrested Jesus—for he was numbered among us and allotted his share in this ministry.' (Now this man acquired a field with the reward of his wickedness; and falling headlong, he burst open in the middle and all his bowels gushed out. This became known to all the residents of Jerusalem, so that the field was called in their language Hakeldama, that is Field of Blood)." (Acts 1:16-19)

The first difference you notice between the two accounts is that in one, Judas is said to have hanged himself, and in the other, he is said to have fallen head first— resulting in his mid-section blowing up. Conservative Christians have gone to great creative lengths to make these two differing legends harmonize with each other—it's usually something about Judas hanging himself, but the rope broke and somehow he fell headlong and his bowels blew out of his midsection—but that is not what I want to focus on here.

I want to focus on two simple points: 1) Matthew says THE PRIESTS purchased the field, while Luke says JUDAS purchased the field; and 2) Matthew says the field got its name because Judas' blood-money was used to purchase it, while Luke says that it got its name because Judas *blew up in a bloody mess* there. But no big deal, right? These are just minor contradictions in the biblical stories about this event or that, right?

But even if you accept that kind of absurd logic about minor details, you have a much bigger problem when it comes to massive contradictions about an event that is very central to Christianity: what happened on the first Easter.

4) The First Easter—What Happened?

After relating the details about Jesus' death and burial, the four gospel writers each relate a narration of events that occurred on that first Easter Sunday morning. And boy, does it get confusing. Professor Bart Ehrman, an excellent voice for those of us who were once evangelicals but are no longer, summarizes the confused and contradictory situation in the Resurrection narratives very well:

"Who actually went to the tomb? Was it Mary alone (John 20:1)? Mary and another Mary (Matt. 28:1)? Mary Magdalene, Mary the mother of James, and Salome (Mark 16:1)? Or women who had accompanied Jesus from Galilee to Jerusalem—possibly Mary Magdalene, Joanna, Mary the Mother of James, and 'other women' (Luke 24:1; see 23:55)? Had the stone already been rolled away from the tomb (as in Mark 16:4) or was it rolled away by an angel while the women were there (Matthew 28:2)? Whom or what did they see there? An angel (Matthew 28:5)? A young man (Mark 16:5)? Two men (Luke 24:4)? Or nothing and no one (John)? And what were they told? To tell the disciples to "go to Galilee," where Jesus will meet them (Mark 16:7)? Or to remember what Jesus had told them 'while he was in Galilee,' that he had to die and rise again (Luke 24:7)? Then, do the women tell the disciples what they saw and heard (Matthew 28:8), or do they not tell anyone (Mark 16:8)? If they tell someone, whom do they tell? The eleven disciples (Matthew 28:8)? The eleven disciples and other people (Luke 24:8)? Simon Peter and another unnamed disciple (John 20:2)? What do the disciples do in response? Do they have no response because Jesus himself immediately appears to them (Matthew 20:9)? Do they not believe the women because it seems to be 'an idle tale' (Luke 24:11)? Or do they go to the tomb to see for themselves (John 20:3)?" (*Jesus, Interrupted*; pp. 48-49)

5) Jesus Exits Earth – But From Where?

Another clearly contradictory post-resurrection narration of events concerns the disagreement among the biblical authors about what the disciples were told by Jesus to do after his death—and the location from which Jesus exited planet earth. Again, Professor Ehrman summarizes the contradiction:

"If Matthew is right, that the disciples immediately go to Galilee and see Jesus ascend from there, how can Luke be right that the disciples stay in Jerusalem the whole time, see Jesus ascend from there, and stay on until the day of Pentecost?" (*op. cit.*, p. 49)

Sadly, the Gospel writers can't even agree on such a central event as the location of Jesus' *bon voyage*!

There are hundreds of other contradictions, discrepancies, and varying viewpoints in the New Testament, but let's have a look at a few in the Old.

The Old Testament

1) How Did King Saul Die?

The unfortunate and oft-maligned first king of Israel, Saul, purportedly died more than once, and by different means, if you believe the biblical text:

In an act of suicide:

"So Saul took his own sword, and fell upon it. When his armor-bearer saw that Saul was dead, he also fell upon his sword and died with him. So Saul and his three sons and his armor-bearer and all his men died together on the same day." (I Sam. 31:4-5)

By the hand of an Amalekite:

"Then David asked the young man who was reporting to him, 'How do you know that Saul and his son Jonathan died?' The young man reporting to him said, 'I happened to be on Mt. Gilboa; and there was Saul leaning on his spear, while the chariots and horsemen drew close to him. When he looked behind him, he saw me, and called to me. I answered, Here sir. And he said to me, Who are you? I answered him, I am an Amalekite. He said to me, come stand over me and kill me; for convulsions have seized me, and yet my life still lingers. So I stood over him, and killed him, for I knew that he could not live after he had fallen." (2 Sam. 1:5-10)

By the Philistines:

"David went and took the bones of Saul and the bones of his son Jonathan from the people of Jabesh-gilead, who had stolen them from the public square of Beth-Shan, where The Philistines had hung them up, on the day the Philistines killed Saul on Gilboa." (2 Sam. 21:12)

By Yahweh himself:

"So Saul died for his unfaithfulness; he was unfaithful to the LORD in that he did not keep the command of the LORD; moreover, he had consulted a medium, seeking guidance, and did not seek guidance from the LORD. Therefore the LORD put him to death and turned the kingdom over to David son of Jesse." (1 Chr. 10:13-14)

Now one might argue (as biblical literalists do) that the words of the Amalekite boy in 2 Sam. 1:5ff were lies that he told King David for his own advantage, but the other statements are incapable of such harmonization. It is clear that here, as in many places in the biblical text, the editors or authors are using differing traditions and show no interest in harmonizing them.

2) Who Caused King David to Take A Census of Israel?

"And the anger of the LORD was kindled against Israel, and he incited David against them, saying, 'Go, count the people of Israel and Judah.'" (2 Sam. 24:1)

"Satan stood up against Israel, and incited David to count the people of Israel." (1 Chr. 21:1)

In the first passage, it is Yahweh who "incited" David to conduct a census. In the second, it is Satan who "incites" him. So which is it? One must only consider that The Chronicler—the author of 1-2 Chronicles who wrote much later than the Deuteronomist (who compiled the books of Samuel)—is not comfortable with the Deuteronomist's account of this census event. Perhaps he was disturbed by the notion that Yahweh would incite David to take a census, and then kill 70,000 Israelites because he did so (21:14). If so, then *voila!*— It wasn't Israel's God who made David do this awful thing, but the Devil! Since the Chronicler was writing somewhere between 400 and 250 CE (there's no consensus on exactly when), when the Satan character was just beginning to figure in the religious thought of the Jews, it's easy to see why he changed the "inciter" of David's census from God to the Devil.

There are massive amounts of contradictions between the Chronicler and the Books of Samuel-Kings, and this example is just the tip of the iceberg (see Helms, *The Bible against Itself*, pp. 15-29).[9]

3) Who Killed Goliath?

Almost everybody has heard the story of David and Goliath. The little righteous guy kills the big bad evil guy who was taunting Israel. But examine the following passages and try to make sense of them:

"David put his hand in his bag, took out a stone, slung it, and struck the Philistine on his forehead; the stone sank into his forehead, and he fell face down on the ground. So David prevailed over the Philistine with a sling and a stone, striking down the Philistine and killing him; there was no sword in David's hand. Then David ran and stood over the Philistine; he grasped his sword, drew it out of its sheath, and killed him; then he cut off his head with it." (1 Sam. 17:49-51)

"Then there was another battle with the Philistines at Gob; and Elhanan son of Jaare-oregim, the Bethlehemite, killed Goliath the Gittite, the shaft of whose spear was like a weaver's beam" (2 Sam. 21:19).

"And there was war with the Philistines; and Elhanan son of Jair killed Lahmi the brother of Goliath the Gittite, the shaft of whose spear was like a weaver's beam." (1 Chr. 20:5).

So, which was it? Did *David*, or *Elhanan*, kill Goliath? In the first passage here it is stated that *David* killed him. In the second, it is said that *Elhanan* did. In the third, it says Elhanan killed the *brother* of Goliath. Trying to harmonize these divergent passages is like trying to juggle chainsaws. But biblical literalists do just that. First they declare that a copyist error must have occurred in the second passage, and it originally read (as in the third passage) "the *brother* of Goliath." The problem is, there are no Hebrew manuscripts in existence that have the "brother" reading. So this is just one of many examples where literalists can't explain the contradiction, so they just say "that's not what was in the original manuscript!"

We might note some other problems with the first passage here. At first, it seems to say that David killed Goliath with only his slingshot. Then, in the next breath, it says he walked over, took Goliath's sword and killed him again. How many times did this poor slob have to be killed by David?

What is much more likely is that several traditions about Goliath's death were floating around during those days (killed by a slingshot; killed by a sword), and the compiler of 1 Samuel included them both. It would also explain the transfer of the person responsible for killing him from the relatively unknown person Elhanan, to King David, the hero of Israel. That is, an earlier tradition credited Elhanan with the kill, but some later compiler transferred the story to the great king.

There are thousands of internal contradictions within the Biblical writings, and these are only a tiny fraction of such discrepancies. Literalists will spare no expense in trying to harmonize them, using tactics like stating "the original manuscripts had something different" (and it's convenient for them that we have none of the "originals"), to using the "any single book may not tell the whole story" nonsense that they often employ with the Four Gospels (e.g., in trying to explain what was written on the placard above Jesus' head on the cross, or in trying to explain what happened on the first Easter). This last tactic employed with the four Gospels requires the reader to construct a *fifth* Gospel, which includes the varying details of an event, to actually get to the "truth" of what happened in any account that has a parallel in another Gospel (see Ehrman, *Jesus Interrupted*, pp. 61-97). Their overall method is clear: They come to the anthology of texts we call The Bible with an overriding presupposition—that there ARE no contradictions in them—and then engage in some of the most absurd and illogical gymnastics to make that seem true. Heck, I could make *any* two books agree (or 66 books, as here) by simply applying that presuppositional methodology. I could even make the Koran and the Bible seem to be totally in sync.

But, so as not to shortchange you on the subject, here is a summary of a few other internal contradictions that you can research:

Is it OK to pray in public, or not? (cf. 1 Tim. 2:8 with Matt. 6:5-6)

Is salvation by faith alone, or by faith and good deeds? (cf. Eph. 2:8-9 with James 2:14-17—and cf. especially 2:24)

Did Jesus say anything to Pilate after his arrest? (cf. Matt. 27:13-14 with John 18:33-37)

Did Moses see God? (cf. Ex. 33:11 with 33:20; cf. also John 1:18)

Has a mere mortal ever ascended into heaven? (cf. John 3:13 with 2 Kings 2:11)

Will the earth last forever? (cf. Eccl. 1:4 with Matt. 24:35)

Did the fig tree cursed by Jesus wither away immediately, or overnight? (cf. Matt. 21:19-20 with Mark 11:13-21)

Did God make known his name "Yahweh" to Abraham or not? (cf. Gen. 15:7 with Exodus 6:3)

There are hundreds of others, and if you want to see just how many, consult the recent publication "The Skeptics Annotated Bible."[10] It's a great resource to get a feel for just how many actual internal Bible discrepancies there are.

THE BIBLE'S SIGNIFICANT DISAGREEMENT WITH SCIENCE

There has long been discussion about whether or not modern science contradicts "religion." This is a conflated question, because there is a difference between asking whether it contradicts *religion* and whether it contradicts *the Bible*. Religion is a fairly broad term which can include many different belief systems. Religions of all kinds generally concern themselves with the existence of a deity (or deities), man's place in the world, and things like salvation, righteous living, prayer, etc. The Bible, on the other hand, is a book—or rather a collection of books—which makes declarative statements about the existence of the Hebrew God "Yahweh," the life of Jesus of Nazareth, and tons of other related subjects.

Things like the existence of a deity, the efficacy of prayer, devils and demons, salvation, sin, and other metaphysical concepts cannot currently be proven or disproven by science. Nor is it science's mission to do so. Science is concerned with gathering, and then interpreting, physical data from the universe. Science cannot answer the question "Does God exist?" —at least at present— because the concept of God is one that does not admit of physical examination.

However, although the Bible makes declarative statements about metaphysical things, it also makes statements about things which *are* testable by science. Things like the age of the earth, the origin of humankind, the global flood, earth's place in the universe, the position and nature of the sun, and other such things. If it can be demonstrated that the Bible is dead wrong about these rather large issues—and it most assuredly is—then why would anyone trust it in other matters (the existence of the Hebrew/Christian God, salvation, sin, demons, etc. etc. etc.?). I will discuss this in much greater detail in Chapter 8. But for now, let's examine just a few of the provable contradictions between science and the Bible.

1) Genesis 1

If you could read Genesis chapter one with no previous scientific knowledge about the universe, you would get the following picture:

God first creates light, and then creates the sun 3 days later (1:3; 1:14ff).

God creates a "dome" (Heb. *raki'a*; 1:6-8),[11] and places this dome in the middle of the watery chaos that is earth. There are thus waters below this dome and waters above it. Picture it this way: You have a flat dinner plate—composed of water—and then you place a round bowl, upside down, on top of it, which actually lifts some of the plate/water on top of it (the author is later going to tell us that the water above the bowl/dome is going to fall back to earth as rain through a "window" in the bowl/dome (in chapter 8, verse 2).

Alright, we have a flat, all-water chaotic and formless earth, and an inverted bowl above it which supports another ocean of water above it.

Then, God gathers all the waters beneath the dome into ONE place, and *voila!* —some dry land appears (1:9).

Next, God creates 3 separate kinds of "lights," and hangs them (presumably) on the underside of the inverted bowl/dome (1:14-18).

These three lights are the sun, the moon, and the stars. The purpose of these lights was to separate the light from the darkness, although according to v. 4 in this same chapter God had already done that on day one (which, by the way, is another contradiction).

After creation of plants, land animals, and birds, he finally creates humankind (1:26), *in his image*. The Hebrew word for "image" is *tselem*, and we may naturally assume that it means a *physical* image (cf. 1 Sam. 6:5; 2 Kings 11:18 where "physical image" is its meaning). This is likely the meaning here, and fits well with what the J-author has God doing in subsequent chapters that suggest he has a physical body like man's—i.e., he walks in the Garden of Eden in the cool of the day, he speaks, he hears things, and he seems limited in knowledge just like man (Gen. 3:8-13).

So there you have it—creation *a la* Genesis. And if you have even a smattering of scientific knowledge about the earth, the sun, and the stars, you can see that this picture is wrong on SO many levels. It is patently absurd, and in case you need some explanation, here's why:

1. The earth is not flat.
2. There is no "firmament" (or "expanse" as some conservative translations try to soften the term) placed over the flat earth. What science and technology have shown us is that the earth is round, or more accurately *a sphere*, and what appeared to the ancients as a rounded firmament (dome) is actually just earth's atmosphere in which light rays are bent in a way to give the appearance of a "blue" dome. They no doubt perceived of the dome as round, because the sun appears to "rise" above one flat horizon and travel in a circular manner until it "sets" (disappears) below the other. Of course, we now know that the sun remains relatively stationary in position while the earth flies around it in an elliptical orbit at about 67,000 miles per hour.
3. The sun, moon, and stars are not "hung" in this firmament (which is non-existent to begin with), as science has enlightened

us about their positions. The moon is about 240,000 miles from earth, the sun is about 93,000,000 miles away, and the nearest stars (excluding the sun, which is actually a star) are 4.2 light years away (Alpha Centauri). What is the distance of 4.2 light years? Somewhere in the neighborhood of 24 *trillion* miles. And the star cluster Alpha Centauri is merely the nearest to us. There are perhaps more than 10,000,000,000,000,000,000,000 stars in the (observable) known universe—-that's ten *sextillion*. That's a bunch of stars, and the mass majority of them are not even in our galaxy. And there are perhaps 100 to 500 *billion* total galaxies in the known universe. So, in short, stars are not "hung" anywhere. They are just "out there" (in relation to our position on earth), and most are enormous gaseous spheres much larger than our sun (ignoring the very numerous "red dwarves" that generally are smaller than our sun and not very luminous).

4. There is no ocean or sea above the earth. This would perhaps be a natural assumption for an ancient, who tried to explain the origin of rain. But the "windows of heaven" don't open (Gen. 8:2) to allow water to fall to the earth. Science has well explained that rain comes from water which evaporates from oceans, seas, lakes, etc. on the earth, which then form clouds of moisture in our atmosphere, and when the water droplets become too dense (and thus heavy) in those clouds they fall back to earth as rain.

5. "Night" and "Day" are not separate occurrences on planet earth. Our days and nights occur because the earth is spinning in a circular motion on its axis, and when half of it faces the sun that half has day, but the other half has night. When it's daytime in America it's night time in China, etc. *At the same time.* It's worth repeating here that the author of Genesis 1 also failed to notice an internal contradiction in his narrative. On day one (Gen 1:4) it is said that God "separated" the light (day) from the darkness (night), but later on day four (Gen. 1:18) it is said that God

"separated" the light (day) from the darkness (night) *by hanging the sun and moon in the firmament.* In other words, he had already separated day from night on the first day, but curiously does it again on the fourth day.

2) The Age of the Earth

In short, the Bible says the earth is about six *thousand* years old (eight or ten thousand, if you *really* stretch it), but science tells us it is more like 4.5 *billion* years old. Quite a difference, I'd say, and an irreconcilable one.

How do we determine that the Bible says the earth is six (or so) thousand years old? It's really quite simple. Genesis 1:1 states that God created the earth on day one, then five days later (on day six) he created Adam (1:26-27). Genesis chapter 5 gives us the genealogy and ages of men from Adam through Noah. Genesis chapter 11 then gives us the genealogy and ages of men from Noah through Abraham. The Gospel of Matthew then gives us a genealogy from Abraham to Jesus. And since we know that Jesus of Nazareth lived somewhere around 6 BCE through about 30 CE, we can pinpoint the Biblical claim for the general age of the earth. Other genealogical details concerning the time between Abraham and Jesus are given in the Books of Kings and Chronicles, but these more or less follow the Genesis genealogies.

And these genealogical records break down as follows:
Adam to Noah > about 1,056 years
Noah to Abraham > about 892 years
Abraham to Jesus > about 2,000 years
Jesus to now > about 2000 years
Add all these up, and *voila!* —you get about 6,000 years!

Now due to some inconsistences in these genealogical records, as well as a few places where intermediate persons in the line are left out, one might conclude that a few more years need to be added to reach an accurate total number of years. But we're certainly not talking about billions of years, or the chronologies would make no sense. Even if you stretch them *real* hard, you *might* come up with one or two thousand years more than the 6,000 they seem to indicate—-but 6,000 is the likely accurate round number.

But what does science say about the earth's age? For some time now the consensus of science is that the earth is about 4.5 billion years old. So it's either quite old, or quite young. We're not quibbling about a few centuries or even millennia here—-the chasm between science's earth and The Bible's earth is about 4 and a half *billion* years.

So how does science arrive at the age of the earth? By a number of ways.

First, by radiometric dating. Dr. James Long characterizes it this way:

"Equipped with this knowledge, scientists can now measure quantities of radioactive elements within the earth's rocks. Researchers have performed this impartial scientific analysis on several thousand rock samples located deep within the fossil columns, and the results are consistently within the billions of years for samples estimated to be this ancient via more primitive dating methods. Although researchers believe that early volcanic activity is responsible for destroying the earth's oldest rocks, we can still be certain that specimens exceeding four billion years in age are very much in existence. Similar to the rocks on the earth, most meteorites eventually finding their way onto our planet date at four billion years as well." (*Biblical Nonsense*, p.70)[12]

Second, by deposits in lakebeds. "The Green River lakes in the western part of the United States deposit one layer of sediment each and every year. Currently there are *millions* of layers of sediment that we can see, which means that they are at least millions of years old. In Japan, Lake Suigetsu has white algae that die each year in the spring and form a layer on the lake bottom. Over the rest of the year, dark clay covers it, forming a light/dark sediment that is repeated over and over each year. There are tens of thousands of such layers that can be seen currently, making the claim that earth is 6-8 thousand years old an absurdity." (*op. cit.*, p. 71)

Third, by the mile-thick layer of permafrost in the Arctic. "We know that it takes decades to form a sheet of this ice even one foot thick. Therefore, this mile-long layer would've taken hundreds of thousands of years to form—not 6 to 8 thousand." (*op. cit.*, p. 72)

Fourth, the use of DNA as a timepiece. Dr. Long again explains:

"In addition to revealing that humans had a common ancestor tens of thousands of years ago, our DNA indicates that we had a much more distant common ancestor with bacteria billions of years in the past." (*op. cit.*, p. 72).

And he closes out the argument for an old earth as proven by science with these simple, but powerful, words:

"While there are several more sources I could reference that would successfully defend the undeniable antiquity of the earth, such as the evidence for numerous magnetic pole reversals in the Atlantic Ocean, I trust that you get the important message from all this data. Simply put, the overwhelming amount of evidence points toward an ancient earth." (*op. cit.*, p.72)

3) The Tower of Babel

In Genesis 11, we are treated to this narrative:

"Now the whole earth had one language and the same words." (v. 1)

"Then they said, 'Come, let us build ourselves a city, and a tower with its top in the heavens." (v.4)

"The Lord came down to see the city and the tower, which mortals had built. And the Lord said, 'Look, they are one people, and they have all one language; and this is only the beginning of what they will do; nothing that they propose to do will now be impossible for them. Come let us go down, and confuse their language there, so that they will not understand one another's speech.'" (vv. 5-7)

Get it? All humankind up to that point, who ALL spoke the same language, decided to build a city and a tower so that they wouldn't be scattered around the then-known world. That is, they wanted to hunker down together, make themselves known and feared, so other (future?) tribes of people wouldn't bother them. But Yahweh (and other gods, angels, heavenly court-members?) said "Let *us* go down" there and confuse their speech, so they can't understand each other and will have to scatter on their own.

There are so many things wrong with this ancient myth—for those who wish to accept it as historical, accurate fact—that I can only begin to point them out. First, the sciences of archaeology and history have clearly shown that there were already many different cultures and languages present in both hemispheres of the earth when this "Tower of Babel" event allegedly occurred (about 2400-2200 BCE, according to Christian literalists):

"The process of sedentarization is first thought to have occurred around 12,000 BCE in the Levant region of southwest Asia though other regions around the world soon followed. The emergence of civilization is generally associated with the Neolithic, or Agricultural Revolution, which occurred in various locations between 8,000 and 5,000 BCE, specifically in southwestern/southern Asia, northern/central Africa and Central America.[23] This revolution marked the beginning of stable agriculture and animal domestication which enabled economies and cities to develop." (*Wikipedia*, "Civilization.")

Second, the "confusion of speech" is no guarantee that people will scatter. The project taken on by these mythical characters—to build a city and a tower for (probably) security reasons—could easily have been completed by them even if they spoke different languages. Language is certainly the easiest means by which to communicate. But there are others—like hand signals, drawing in the dirt, teaching a few basic words of your language to the other fellow, etc. If Yahweh caused every single one of them to speak a different language (tens of thousands at this point?—the text DOES say "the whole earth," implying there were quite a large number of people involved here), the task would be difficult. But if he just caused groups of people to suddenly speak a different language, the people in those groups would've been able to understand the language of their group, and work could've resumed.

Of course, as with many biblical texts, the details are not provided. Perhaps this is a function of the editors using the traditions much as they found them and not thinking too deeply about the logical fallacies involved in them. At any rate, current studies in linguistics suggest that there never was a *single* language that birthed all the others, but that civilizations in various parts of the world developed their own with the evolution of time. And thus, the story of the Tower of Babel is just another myth that found its way into the Bible, and while it reflects some of the cultural realities of the day, it is completely false on the facts.

There are hundreds of other places where declarative statements in the Bible contradict what is known from science, but these should suffice to indicate that while science and *religion* may have few points of disagreement, science and *the Bible* have many. And of course many people base their religion upon the Bible. But for those of you who would like a few more examples, here is a selective summary:

The earth does not "sit on foundations," as the ancients believed (1 Sam. 2:8; 2 Sam. 22:16; I Chr. 16:13; Job 9:16, etc.).

The earth does not have an "end" anywhere, since it's a sphere (Isa. 5:26). It also does not have "four corners" (Isa. 11:12).

Stars cannot "fall" from the sky, which assumes that earth is stationary and stars are suspended above it (Isa. 34:4; Mark 13:24-25, etc.). Plus, if a star (and our sun is a star) ever got *near* the earth—even one of them—earth would vaporize in short order.

There was never any global flood in the days of Noah (Gen. 6-9). The geologic record shows evidence of all kinds of local flooding events, but no evidence whatsoever of this worldwide cataclysmic covering of the whole earth with water. Plus there are historic records from many other cultures which date from before, during, and after the supposed time of the flood—none of which mention any such *worldwide* cataclysm. And if such an event had occurred one would expect a considerable gap in those records—since all these nations would've been destroyed—but no such gap exists. They read as if the earth continued with business as usual. And that, of course, is because it did.

There are hundreds of other examples, and again I encourage you to look at *The Skeptic's Annotated Bible* for examples of where science and the Bible are irreconcilable (endnote #10.).

So we return to the main question posed by this chapter: What is the Bible, REALLY? A simple, and rational, answer to this question is as follows:

The Bible, whether the Protestant, Catholic, or Eastern Orthodox form of it, is simply a collection of books that arose out of ancient Hebrew culture to explain the perceived dealings of their God, "Yahweh," with his people (Old Testament) and to explain the life and significance of Jesus of Nazareth (New Testament)—much as the Koran explains the God Allah to his people, and the significance of the prophet Muhammad.

And while it is an extremely interesting anthology of writings, and one to which I have devoted a good part of my life to studying (much as I have to other literature), perhaps it is more important to consider what it is *not*:

1) It is not a word-by-word message from any deity to the inhabitants of earth. If you accept that it is, then you must concede that this deity is extremely confused (e.g., he can't even get the parallel accounts of historical events to agree), and is

totally unaware of the actual construction of the universe (the earth is not flat, it is not 6 to 8 thousand years old, rain doesn't drip down through the windows of heaven, etc. etc.). In short, if "God" wrote this "book," we're all in a world of hurt. He is stupid, non-precise, and unable to perceive his own universe. And not only that, but he has a bundle of bad character traits previously referred to in this book (jealousy, blood-thirstiness, deceitfulness, etc. etc.).

2) It is not a "book." It is a *collection* of books—a library, if you will—with differing viewpoints about God and history, wisdom and prophecy, and life in general.

3) It is not a "book of theology." Theology, in general, is the attempt by persons of various faith communities to neatly organize the massive amounts of statements in the Bible into a coherent and harmonious whole—by topic. For example, if you read Calvin's *Institutes* (one of the more famous and influential theologies composed by John Calvin in the 16th Century), you will find a section on "God," one on "sin," one on "predestination," etc. It can be said that these various theologies have replaced the Bible as the authority in the various churches. "Biblical Inerrancy" or "Sola Scriptura" (Scripture Only) may be the cry of the conservative Christian church, but the various theologies are the real drivers of their belief systems.

4) It is not a "book for children." You only have to read through the Old Testament one time to see the references to incest, sorcery, adultery, rape, slavery, barbarianism (e.g., the gouging out of eyes, cutting off of bodily appendages, the slaughter of women and children, genocide, racism, executions by fire, stonings, etc.), and other things to see that it is not something to which a 7 year old needs to be exposed. Though less so in the New Testament, there are equally non-children-friendly references to infanticide, torture, capital punishment, demons, self-mutilation, etc.

So now that we have that out of the way, we'll consider the next supposed witness to divine matters —the Church.

ENDNOTES

1) "The Chicago Statement on Biblical Inerrancy," put together by a broad range of evangelical Christians, is regarded as representative of what inerrantists believe. Its general attitude about the Bible is contained in point #4 of the "Short Statement" that appears at its beginning:

"4. Being wholly and verbally God-given, Scripture is without error or fault in all its teaching, no less in what it states about God's acts in creation, about the events of world history, and about its own literary origins under God, than in its witness to God's saving grace in individual lives."

The Catholics have a similar doctrinal statement about the Bible in the Vatican II decree "Dei Verbum."

2) A "canon" of Scripture is a list of books regarded to be divinely inspired by a religious group. Judaism regards the 24 (= Christian 39) books of the Old Testament as their canon, Protestants regard the 66 books of the Old and New Testaments as their canon, and Catholics regard the 66 books of the Protestant Old and New Testaments, plus several others, as their canon. The Eastern Orthodox Church has essentially the same canon as the Catholics do, with some minor differences. "Canon" comes from the Greek word *kanon*, which means "measuring stick" or "rule."

3) E.L. James, Vintage Books, 2011

4) Some very excellent surveys on church history include *Church History in Plain Language,* Bruce L. Shelley, 2008 (Thomas Nelson); *A History of Christianity,* Paul Johnson, 1976 (Touchstone). Anything written by Bart D. Ehrman or Bishop John Shelby Spong provide very readable and scholarship-based glimpses into church history. If you want to read something that is very close to the early events of the Christian movement, go back and peruse Eusebius' *Ecclesiastical History,* written at the beginning of the 4th Century CE.

5) From the late 1800's until a few decades ago the closing of the Old Testament canon was assumed to have occurred at the Council of Jamnia in the late 1st Century CE, but this theory is no longer accepted by most scholars. There is currently no consensus as to exactly when it may have been considered to be closed.

6) *Forged: Writing in the Name of God*--Why the Bible's Authors Are Not Who We Think They Are (HarperOne), 2011.

7) Ehrman, *op. cit.*

8) *Jesus, Interrupted:* Revealing the Hidden Contradictions in the Bible (And Why We Don't Know About Them). HarperOne, 2009.

9) *The Bible Against Itself:* Why the Bible Seems To Contradict Itself. Randel McCraw Helms (Millennium Press, 2006).

10) The *Skeptic's Annotated Bible*: The King James Version from a skeptic's point of view. Annotated by Steve Wells. (SAB Books, 2013)

11) The Hebrew verb root rq^c means ""to beat out, spread out", e.g., as in the process of making a dish or bowl by hammering thin a lump of metal.

12) *Biblical Nonsense*—A Review of the Bible for Doubting Christians. Dr. Jason Long (iUniverse, Inc., 2005).

Chapter Six
WHAT IS THE CHURCH, REALLY?

If you are a Christian, it's likely that you regard one of two possible things as your source of authority for your beliefs--either The Bible or your church. More specifically, if you are a Protestant evangelical you regard that authority as the Bible, and if you're Catholic the Church is your guide. Of course, in real life there is not such a formal practical distinction in the everyday lives of Christians, since Protestant evangelicals also often look to their local church for their understanding of the Bible and their faith.

But it's still true that the main formal difference between the two groups is that one (Protestant evangelicals) venerate the Bible as their last word on faith and practice, and the other (Catholics) regard the church—or more specifically the infallible declarations of the succession of Popes—as their last word on faith and practice.

We have looked at the Bible in the previous chapter, and now we will look at the Catholic Church. Both are claimed as infallible witnesses to metaphysical truth by these two main groups of Christians in America, and my purpose here is to examine this second "witness," as it were. We will ask, "Is the Papal succession (as reflected in statements by the Vatican) a consistent and trustworthy source for determining the existence and working of things like Heaven, Hell, Demons, the Devil, etc., or not?"

It would be impossible in this book to set out the entire history of the "church" since Jesus' time, because it contains about 2,000 years of events occurring over a wide geography. It is an evolving and varied history, and one littered with acts of brutality. At some points up to the present, the governing powers of the state have controlled it, and at others the church has controlled the state. But there are many good resources for studying this history (see Endnote #4, Chapter 5), if the reader is inclined to understand more.

My purpose here is to examine whether Witness Number Two—the Catholic Church—is a reliable source when it comes to stating what "lies behind the curtain" of our physical world. I will begin by offering a ridiculously short summary of how the church got started, and then focus specifically on whether or not this history should elicit a trusting response in the believer.

It is perhaps a little-known fact by the average American that Jesus never went to church, was anywhere near a church, or even had any inkling about how the "church" would evolve in the (now) 2000 years since his time on earth. The obvious reason for this is that there *was* no such organization while he was here. In certain of the four canonical Gospels, he is portrayed as saying things like "You are Peter, and upon this rock (i.e., Peter) I will build my church, and the gates of Hell will not prevail against it (Matt. 16:18)." But even if he did say something like that at some time during his life, he says precious little about any such institution anywhere else. Many scholars have thus concluded that he had no idea he would be responsible for such a new and non-Judaic organism as what we now know as *the church*.

But in order to understand the Catholic Church—the only form of the church that existed for the first sixteen centuries after Jesus—a *very* short summary of its history is in order.

The very first followers of Jesus were all Jews, and followed Judaism with its laws of circumcision, diet, and other codes. They believed that Jesus was the promised Messiah (Christ) from their Scriptures (what Christians now call the Old Testament), but most of them believed that adherence to Old Testament Judaism was still necessary for salvation. They also still attended local synagogues, and it seems clear that at some point the synagogue authorities threw them out. They were no doubt thrown out for their constant reading of parts of the Old Testament which they claimed were prophecies predicting Jesus of Nazareth as the long-awaited "Messiah" of Israel. It was the custom in many synagogues for members of the congregation to get up and read parts of the Old Testament during gatherings, but these new Jesus-followers went a step further. They would read a certain passage, claim it was a prophecy, and then claim that Jesus was the fulfillment of it and that the congregants should acknowledge his Messiahship. These believers in Jesus came to be known collectively in some of these synagogues as "The Way" (Acts 9:2), and were expelled universally by Judaism probably during the years 80-90 CE.

From Jerusalem these early Jesus adherents spread out northward (Syria), eastward (Mesopotamia), and westward (Asia Minor, Egypt, etc.), and into the Roman Empire as a whole, spreading their message about Jesus. This very early period has been dubbed "The Apostolic Period," because it primarily designates the history of Christianity during which the Apostles were still alive (roughly 35-100 CE). During this period many quarrels about core beliefs emerged, such as whether or not one had to both believe in Jesus and keep the Old Testament law to be "saved," or whether simple belief in Jesus was enough. During this early period there were sporadic persecutions also, both by Jewish authorities and on a larger scale by the Roman authorities (cf. Emperor Nero's rash of persecutions, based on his public claim that the Christians had started the Great Fire of Rome; it is possible that the writing of the Book of Revelation was motivated by Nero's harsh treatment of Christians).

During the next few centuries, often referred to as the "Post-Apostolic Period" (roughly 100 CE to about 380 CE), the church evolved into a much more formally organized institution. There came into existence the formal offices of bishops, elders, overseers, and deacons (derived from the more loose use of the terms mentioned in the apostolic writings—the New Testament). The notion of "apostolic succession" — that the authority of a bishop was derived from a straight line back to the apostles—was developed during this time. And since Peter was regarded as the prime apostle (remember Jesus' alleged words in Matt. 16:18, "You are Peter, and upon this rock I will build my church"), the idea of a Papacy was beginning to take shape. Peter was the "first Pope," according to later Catholic doctrine, and every Pope since is regarded as having Petrine authority. This is why, in Catholic tradition, the Pope can make "infallible" pronouncements about God and church doctrine, even if those pronouncements seem to be at odds with various parts of the Bible.

The post-apostolic period also saw the emergence of at least three main schools of thought about Christianity. As mentioned before, these may be broadly categorized as "proto-orthodox," "Gnostic," and "Ebionite."[1] The proto-orthodox group began to develop organized religious dogma that eventually became the accepted or "orthodox" form of Christianity that survives to this day. This is largely due to the fact that when the Roman Empire decreed Christianity to be the state religion, it also refereed the various church councils and declared proto-orthodoxy as the true and official form of the religion. The Gnostics, who had quite a different take on Christ and his purpose, and the Ebionites, who believed that adherence to the laws of Judaism was also necessary for Christians, were declared to be "heretics," and much of their literature and influence were destroyed. If the vote had gone in favor of either of these two groups, our Christianity would look quite different today.

As time passed into the Middle Ages, the history of the church became quite complex and volatile. As Christianity spread into ever-widening areas of Europe, there were geographical schisms, skirmishes for power, varying relationships between church and state, and an evolving notion of Papal authority. It was during this time, specifically in the 11th Century, that a major schism culminated leading to a major split between the church forces in the West and those in the East. This was the origin of the Greek, or Eastern Orthodox Church, which remains as a major division of the religion today. They are not beholden to the Pope, and have their own church hierarchy.

As time passed in the 16th Century, another more significant schism occurred within the Church. Foreshadowed by earlier scholars like John Wycliff and Jan Hus, a Catholic friar named Martin Luther led a revolt against the Catholic Church with the publication of his *95 Theses* in 1517. Meanwhile, the Swiss academic Ulrich Zwingli developed a theology that was much like Luther's, and between the two of them the Protestant Reformation was initiated. Both men had serious issues with both the corruption in Catholic Church hierarchy, as well as with Catholic doctrine. They emphasized that the Bible alone should be the source of religious authority (i.e., *sola scriptura*), and that salvation was by "faith alone" (*sola fide*)—not, as Catholic doctrine stated, by a progressive infusion of grace accepted through faith and cooperated with through man's good works. Second generation reformers, such as John Calvin, further developed this "faith alone" theme with ever-detailed theological treatises. The Catholic religion survived, however, and they launched a "counter-Reformation" of sorts to address some of their internal problems.

The rest of church history from the 16th century to the present is fraught with battles between Catholics and Protestants, Protestants and Protestants, and overall battles between the church and state. Protestant infighting often was accompanied by expulsions, torture, and even executions.

Christianity made its way to America in the 16th Century, and in various forms (Catholics, Puritans, Anglicans, etc.). And it is still a fragmented religion within our borders. For example, one need only look on a street corner where a Southern Baptist church sits with a sign declaring "Once saved, always saved," while on the opposite street corner the Free-Will Baptist church sign reads "Not so fast, Newton! You can have salvation, but you can also lose it!!" Consider also the doctrinal differences within the Catholic Church (e.g., fringe Catholic groups which reject absolute Vatican authority), and within the manifold denominations that have evolved out of the Protestant Reformation (Lutherans, Methodists, Baptists, Presbyterians, Assemblies of God, Mennonites, etc. etc. etc.!). *There is no such thing as a single, monolithic "Christianity,"* and if someone tells you he or she is a Christian, that could mean any number of different things.

But my intent here is not to get bogged down in the minutiae of Christian history, but rather to address the distinct nature of Catholic religion—which claims Papal authority dating back to Peter the Apostle—and more specifically to examine whether or not the "infallible truth of God" claim for official Papal pronouncements is a claim worthy of belief. Remember, both Protestantism and Catholicism regard the Bible as "Scripture," but unlike Protestantism the Catholic position is that the Bible is ultimately to be interpreted only by the Catholic Church.

Papal infallibility was not formulated as an official doctrine of the church until the middle of the 16th century, but the doctrine itself declares that it was in force from the very first "Pope" (The Apostle Peter, if you will) to the present. The infallibility doctrine states that all formal pronouncements made by a Pontiff about faith and morals are the absolute truth of God. However, as we will see in the following examples, the "truth of God" seems subject to change over time with the Catholics. These changes have been caused mostly by the progressive advancement of scientific knowledge, as well as a more ecumenical and tolerant view of religious matters.

HUMAN EVOLUTION.

Darwin's concept of human evolution was first stated in the middle of the 19th Century. Prior to that time, all Christian faiths accepted the notion that on the 6th day of creation God created Adam, then Eve from Adam's rib. This was not understood to be a long drawn out creative act over millions of years, but one which was instantaneous. However, the "evolution" of Catholic teaching on this subject can begin to be seen from various pronouncements by Popes in the 20th Century:

1) <u>Pope Pius X</u>. In 1909, Pius ratified a statement of the Pontifical Biblical Commission that stated that the literal historical meaning of the first chapters of Genesis could not be doubted in regard to "the creation of all things by God at the beginning of time; the special creation of man; the formation of the first woman from the first man; the unity of the human race....".
2) <u>Pope Pius XII</u>. In his 1950 encyclical *Humani Generis*, however, Pius seemed to be opening the door to acceptance of human evolution with various statements. They can be summarized as follows:

    A - The question of the origin of man's body from pre-existing and living matter is a legitimate matter of inquiry for natural science. Catholics are free to form their own opinions, but they should do so cautiously; they should not confuse fact with conjecture, and they should respect the Church's right to define matters touching on Revelation.

    B - Catholics must believe, however, that the human soul was created immediately by God. Since the soul is a spiritual substance it is not brought into being through transformation of matter, but directly by God, whence the special uniqueness of each person.

    C - All men have descended from an individual, Adam, who has transmitted original sin to all mankind. Catholics may not, therefore, believe in "polygenism", the scientific hypothesis that mankind descended from a group of original humans (i.e., that there were many Adams and Eves).

Some theologians believe Pius XII explicitly excludes belief in polygenism as legitimate. The relevant sentence is this:

"Now it is in no way apparent how such an opinion (polygenism) can be reconciled with that which the sources of revealed truth and the documents of the Teaching Authority of the Church propose with regard to original sin, which proceeds from a sin actually committed by an individual Adam and which, through generation, is passed on to all and is in everyone as his own." (Pius XII, *Humani Generis*, 37 and the footnote refers to *Romans* 5:12–19; Council of Trent, Session V, Canons 1–4).

In other words, when it comes to where we all came from, Pius seems to be the first who allows his parishioners to form their own opinions about the subject, *but at the same time* states that there was a *real* Adam who committed the original sin that plunged us all into the sinfulness that results in the need for a Savior from it.

3) <u>Pope John Paul II</u>. In 1996, this Pope made the following statement:

"In his encyclical *Humani Generis* (1950), my predecessor Pius XII has already affirmed that there is no conflict between evolution and the doctrine of the faith regarding man and his vocation, provided that we do not lose sight of certain fixed points.... Today, more than a half-century after the appearance of that encyclical, some new findings lead us toward the recognition of evolution as more than a hypothesis. In fact it is remarkable that this theory has had progressively greater influence on the spirit of researchers, following a series of discoveries in different scholarly disciplines. The convergence in the results of these independent studies—which was neither planned nor sought—constitutes in itself a significant argument in favor of the theory."[2]

In the same address, however, John Paul II rejected any theory of evolution that provides a materialistic explanation for the human *soul*:

"Theories of evolution which, because of the philosophies which inspire them, regard the spirit either as *emerging* from the forces of living matter, or as a simple epiphenomenon of that matter, are incompatible with the truth about man."

4) <u>Pope Benedict</u>. In 1995, Cardinal Ratzinger (before he became Pope Benedict) made this statement:

"The theory of evolution does not invalidate the faith, nor does it corroborate it. But it does challenge the faith to understand itself more profoundly and thus to help man to understand himself and to become increasingly what he is: the being who is supposed to say Thou to God in eternity."[3]

So, dear reader, do you get it? For the "infallible" Papacy the truth about such fundamental religious matters as the origin of man is subject to the evolving conclusions of science. *This is, in all candor, simply nonsense.* Man either had his beginnings six to eight thousand years ago, or *he did not.* You cannot believe in Adam and Eve AND the theory of evolution—-which puts man's origins at about seven million years ago (i.e., the Hominids).

But let's have a look at more evolving truth from our Catholic friends.

SALVATION.

If the succession of Popes from Peter is a guarantee that their pronouncements are the very truth of God and thus immutable, one would expect to find consistency in such central matters as how one can be saved. That is, are we expected to believe that God changes his mind every few centuries or so about so fundamental a matter?

Note these pronouncements by two medieval Popes:

1) Pope Boniface VIII (1294-1303 CE):

"With faith urging us we are forced to believe and to hold the one, holy, Catholic Church and that, apostolic, and we firmly believe and simply confess this (Church) outside which there is no salvation nor remission of sin ... Furthermore, we declare, say, define and proclaim to every human creature that they by necessity for salvation are entirely subject to the Roman Pontiff."[4]

If that's not clear enough, consider the decree of:

2) Pope Eugenius IV (1431-1447):
"It (the Roman Church) firmly believes, professes, and proclaims that those not living within the Catholic Church, not only pagans, but also Jews and heretics and schismatics cannot become participants in eternal life ... and that no one, whatever almsgiving he has practiced, even if he has shed blood for the name of Christ, can be saved, unless he has remained in the bosom and unity of the Catholic Church." (Council of Florence (1441), Pope Eugenius, Decree for the Jacobites, in the Bull Cantata Domino; Denzinger, *op. cit.*, p. 714).

In other words, these early Pontiffs believed and declared that formal membership in, and adherence to the teachings of, the Catholic Church were necessary for salvation. Note that Eugenius even says that if you give significant alms (money to the poor) or shed your blood on behalf of Christ, you cannot be saved unless you "remain in the bosom and unity of the Catholic Church." Pretty clear, wouldn't you say?

But hold on. Fast forward to more modern times and the publishing of the new *Catechism of the Catholic Church*, which declares:

"Outside the Church there is no salvation." But then goes to clarify:

846. "How are we to understand this affirmation, often repeated by the Church Fathers? Re-formulated positively, it means that all salvation comes from Christ the Head through the Church which is his Body..." BUT

847. "This affirmation is not aimed at those who, through no fault of their own, do not know Christ and his Church............Those who, through no fault of their own, do not know the Gospel of Christ or his Church, but who nevertheless seek God with a sincere heart, and, moved by grace, try in their actions to do his will as they know it through the dictates of their conscience - those too may achieve eternal salvation." (*Catechism of the Catholic Church*, Doubleday: New York, © 1994, United States Catholic Conference, Inc. - Libreria Editrice Vaticana, p. 244 w/Imprimi Potest of Cardinal Joseph Ratzinger).

See the problem? In earlier times, membership in the church and subjection to the Pontiff was an absolute necessity to get you into Heaven, but now even those who have never heard of Jesus and The Church can make it also—-*if they follow the dictates of their conscience.* That opens the door for all kinds of non-Catholics to join in Heaven's bliss. In fact, just now—in July of 2013—Pope Francis has opined something that seems nearly unimaginable in this regard. In a sermon to the attendees inside the Chapel Santa Marta on Vatican grounds he uttered these words:

"The Lord has redeemed all of us, all of us, with the Blood of Christ: all of us, not just Catholics. Everyone! 'Father, the atheists?' Even the atheists. Everyone! And this Blood makes us children of God of the first class. We are created children in the likeness of God and the Blood of

Christ has redeemed us all. And we all have a duty to do good. And this commandment for everyone to do good, I think, is a beautiful path towards peace. If we, each doing our own part, if we do good to others, if we meet there, doing good, and we go slowly, gently, little by little, we will make that culture of encounter: We need that so much. We must meet one another doing good. 'But I don't believe, Father, I am an atheist!' But do good: We will meet one another there."

Francis was constructing a hypothetical conversation between an atheist and a parish priest, and he clearly states that even an atheist who "does good" can make the grade. How different this is from the attitude demonstrated by Eugenius or even Boniface VIII cited above!

Of course, a Vatican spokesperson quickly jumped in after this statement and "clarified" it, reiterating traditional Catholic dogma that "people who know the Catholic Church cannot be saved if they refuse to enter or remain in her." But who's the Holy Padre here? The Vatican spokesperson is not the successor to Peter. The Pope—Pope Francis in this case— is (according to Catholic doctrine).

So, once again, we see Catholic dogma, as communicated by the Pope, changing—even on such a central issue as salvation. And if the Papacy is the conduit between heaven and earth, are we to believe that God is changing his truth as time passes? That's a leap no rational person could make.

There are many other issues—such as the nature of the Trinity, Transubstantiation (i.e., the communion wine and bread become Christ's *actual* body and blood), and divorce, for example—-which have undergone modifications since the days of Peter, but you get the point with these brief examples. If God's truth is immutable and unchangeable, and the Pope is the voice of God to earth's inhabitants, then we would expect to see absolutely no change with regard to any doctrine at all. And to be fair, The Church says that none has ever occurred. But the facts say otherwise.

I must interject here that, relative to his predecessors, I really like Pope Francis. He seems to be quite the humble man, and his much more tolerant views about things like salvation, the gays, and the poor are a breath of fresh air from the Catholic camp. But tolerance and humility do not qualify as proof that he speaks for God. He does not, and the ever-changing views of the Catholic Church over time prove that, as a witness to the metaphysical, this church fails miserably.

Let me conclude by saying that Protestant evangelicals are often guilty of the same practice as their Catholic counterparts. That is, the average Christian attends a local church, and often derives his set of beliefs from the Pastor or other authority figure. That pastor or authority figure has usually derived his overall system of beliefs from the doctrinal statement of his or her denomination or group, and those doctrinal statements often originate from one of the Protestant reformers. The difference is—at least in theory—that the individual evangelical pastor or parishioner is free to disagree with his/her denomination's doctrine if he or she believes there is biblical justification for doing so.

So what does all of this mean for those of us who are faced with trying to figure out what we should believe about religious matters in general? We are about to see in the next chapter.

ENDNOTES

1) *Jesus, Interrupted*; pp. 191-198. Ehrman adds the Marcionites as a fourth group.
2) In his "Message to the Pontifical Academy of Sciences: On Evolution"
3) *Dogma And Preaching,* Applying Christian Doctrine to Daily Life; p.142. (Ignatius Press), 2011.
4) *The Sources of Catholic Dogma,* Henry Denzinger (CreateSpace Independent Publishing Platform), 2013; pp. 468-469.

Chapter Seven
WHY IT'S TOTALLY IRRATIONAL TO BELIEVE THIS STUFF

As I have noted earlier, about 7 in 10 American citizens claim to be Christian. You get no hesitation from them when you ask the "yes or no" question "Are you a Christian," but if you go further and ask, "WHY are you a Christian," you're likely to get a slight pause in response. And then, of course, you get the usual menu of answers: e.g., "Cause Jesus changed my life," "Cause I believe in the Bible," "Cause I was raised Baptist," "Cause I'm American," "Cause it makes me feel better about life," etc. etc. etc.

While I don't doubt the sincerity of most of these people in their responses, I do suggest that the "WHY" in their responses is completely flawed. The responses are mostly based on experience or environment, and in no way address the *real* question, "Is Christianity true?" In other words, a belief system can often personally help you navigate life's choppy waters, but that is no proof whatsoever that it is *true*.

What Does It Mean For Something To Be True?

The definition I would use here is a simple one. Something is true *if it corresponds to reality*. If I say that there is a divine being living on Mars, I have made a declarative statement. If such a being actually exists and lives on Mars, then my statement is true. If that being does not exist, then my statement is false. I am using "true" and "false" in the way we speak in the ordinary language of our experience. In other words, there can't *be* a Divine Martian and *not be* a Divine Martian at the same time. He/she/it either exists, or he/she/it doesn't.

In the same way, Christianity—in all of its forms—makes declarative statements about all kinds of things—the existence of the God Yahweh, His divine son Jesus, Hell, Heaven, Sin, Demons, The Devil, and many such things.

So, as intelligent beings, we ought to ask ourselves the question, "Are these things true?" "Do they exist?" In other words, is there an actual place or entity—either in space/time or outside of it—known as Hell?" It either exists, or it does not. Similarly, we should ask the same questions about The Devil, Demons, Sin, Heaven, Angels, or a future Armageddon, Antichrist, and so forth. They either do, or do not exist (or will or will not, in the case of future claims). You can't have it both ways.

If we answer these questions with a "yes, they do exist," then as intelligent beings we ought to have a reason for our belief in them. If someone approaches me on the street and says, "On Friday of this week the entire global economy is going to collapse, and every mode of currency or type of asset will be completely worthless," I will immediately want to know the proof for his claim. If he hands me a paper tract that is published by a fringe conspiracy group, I will immediately examine that tract to see if there is any truth to it. If I find that the "facts" set out in the tract are not facts at all, but rather speculations not based on any empirical evidence, then I should and will decide that this predicted economic collapse is merely an illusion. Friday will come and go, and the world's economy will continue as is.

In this example we have a rough parallel to Christianity and the purported witnesses to its truthfulness. We have examined the two main witnesses for the supernatural and metaphysical claims for the truth of

Christianity—the Bible and the Church—and found them both to be *not credible*. The Bible is 1) internally inconsistent and contradictory, and 2) in conflict with established science. The Church has changed its doctrines about salvation and man's origin—as well as many other things. Therefore, neither one of these self-styled witnesses to the truth of Christianity are worthy of our belief. To expand on this, what we have in the Bible is a collection of "books" written or edited over a period of about 1000 years, wherein both history claims and claims about the physical universe are demonstrably false. And what we have in the Church is an institution in which "truth" has evolved over a period of about 2,000 years. If there were a supreme being either writing the Bible or guiding a church's pronouncements, we should expect *consistency*. But there is none. This is because both the Bible and the Church are the creations of human beings, and not of a divine being.

Let me put it in a more personal way. If you are a Christian, or are contemplating becoming one, I will assume that you have never personally *seen* God, Hell, Heaven, The Devil, Angels, Demons, or the like. These are things that are ostensibly beyond our ability to see, hear, smell, or touch. They are "*meta*physical," or "beyond our physical world." If you have never seen any of these things, why do you (or do you want to) believe in them? You may say, "Because the Bible tells me about them," or "because my Church tells me about them." But do you really want to base your beliefs and your entire life upon a "book" that has been proven to the fair mind to be completely untrustworthy when it comes to its declarations about truth? Or on a church that relies upon that book for its teachings? That book can't even agree, within its pages, about what happened with very important events like the first Easter, or whether salvation is gained by faith—or faith *and* good deeds. And dozens of alleged historical narratives contained in it contradict each other, leaving the reader to only surmise what actually may have happened (if anything at all actually did in any given case). Even Jesus himself, if you read the

Gospels without pre-conceived notions, seems like a different person from one book to the next (e.g., compare the Jesus in the Gospel of Mark versus the one in John).

And not only that, we don't even have the original writings of the Bible. In the case of the New Testament, for example, the closest full version of it (to the original) that we possess comes from more than 300 years after Jesus lived—longer than America has been in existence! And no single manuscript copy we possess matches the composite Greek text scholars have put together which underlies the English (or other) translation of it that we actually read. The Bible-believer must believe that God took care to inspire each and every word that the original writers penned, and then was essentially "hands off" when it came to the copying phase that allowed all those books to get beyond the original composition and distribution of them. Seems a little more than odd, don't you think? That is, the eternal God had a message for mankind, so he communicated it in individual writings by various persons over 1000 years, but when it came to getting that very important message to the mass of mankind, he allowed all kinds of mistakes, corruptions, scribal "text-tampering" and the like to occur—that is, until the invention of the printing press in the 16th Century CE (1500 or so years after the latest biblical documents were written). That's a bridge *way* too far for any reasonable person, I think.

Further oddities in such a dogma (biblical inerrancy) have to do with the actual languages and texts themselves. For example, the original Hebrew text of the Old Testament was written without vowels (vowel pointings), which did not exist in Hebrew at the time the Old Testament documents were written (see Figs. 1-2). These vowel pointings were mostly added by the Masoretes (a group of medieval Hebrew scholars), around the 9th and 10th Centuries CE—nearly two thousand years after the earliest Hebrew parts of the Old Testament were written. Of course, a great majority of the text is not in question as to each author's original intent, but there are a significant number of places where pointing the text with different vowels would change the meaning (e.g., 1 Sam. 8:16; Gen. 49:10). So this omission of the vowels is somewhat odd, wouldn't you say, if God were concerned about the perfect revelation contained in each and every word? And worse than that—for those who claim the divine inspiration of the Bible, that is—is that a number of sections of the Old Testament are not even written in Hebrew! They are written in Aramaic—a language closely related to Hebrew, but a separate and distinct language nonetheless (Gen. 31:47 – translation of a Hebrew place-name; Jer. 10:11 – a single sentence denouncing idolatry occurring in the middle of a Hebrew text; Dan. 2:4b–7:28 – five stories about Daniel and his colleagues, plus an apocalyptic vision; and the narratives in Ezra 4:8–6:18 and 7:12–26). What? Are we supposed to believe that the eternal God was composing away in Hebrew, then at random and seemingly unprovoked moments he lapsed into Aramaic? Please! This is beyond credulity for any rational person.

*Fig. 1. This is a section of the Great Isaiah Scroll discovered in 1947 in the caves near the Dead Sea (the Dead Sea Scrolls). It dates to about 125 BCE, and is an example of Hebrew written **without** vowel markings.*

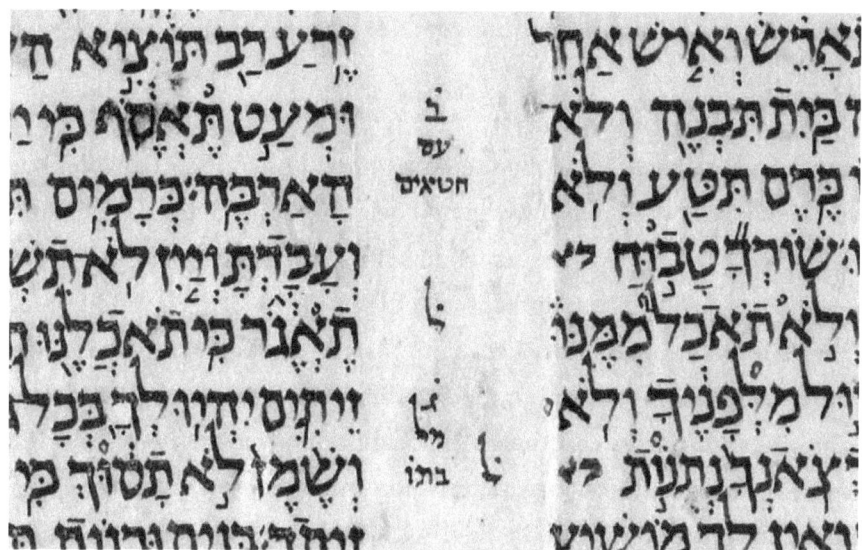

*Fig. 2. This is a section (Josh. 1:1) of the Aleppo Codex, which re-emerged in 1958 after being shuffled around in various historical conflicts. It dates to the 10th Century CE, and is an example of Hebrew written **with** vowel markings.*

The obvious rational answer to this language switching issue is that certain biblical copyists in later times switched the language from Hebrew to what their audience could understand—Aramaic. Or perhaps the copyist himself was beginning to lose fluency in Hebrew and went with his "first" language in certain places. Not hard to imagine, since after Hebrew began to pass out of common use beginning in the 5th Century BCE, Aramaic gradually became the language of the common Hebrew people.

Add to this the fact that the New Testament documents were written in 1st century ("Koine") Greek, which was generally not written with spaces between words or with punctuation (see Fig. 3). An English example will suffice to illustrate this:

todayisfridayandtheforecastisforcloudyskiesandrain

Now, to be fair, most of the intended word separations in the New Testament are clear enough, but there are a number of places where the original intended word division is not clear, and a phrase can be divided or punctuated in more than one way (e.g., with either a "period" or a "question mark".)

Another phenomenon is worth mentioning here, although it is a more modern one. Originally there was no enumeration of chapters or verses in any of the biblical writings. Their final original forms consisted of individual books that were intended to be read as a whole—e.g., all of Galatians, all of 1st Thessalonians, all of Chronicles, etc. The addition of "verse" numbering did not occur until the 16th Century, and it has done more to confuse biblical understanding than to enhance it. Few Christians nowadays read entire biblical books, but single out specific "verses" which are then given a stand-alone meaning. Such a verse is often ripped from the context of the book as a whole and given an importance and meaning

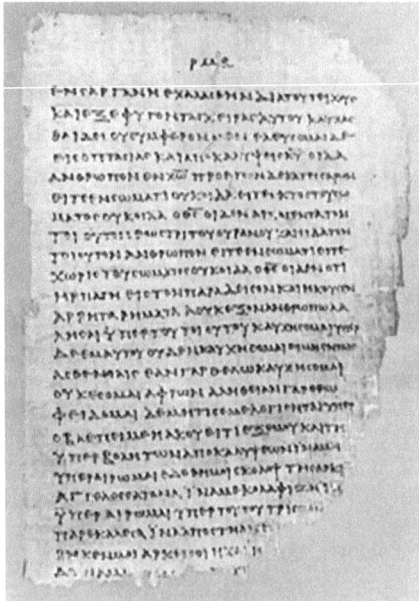

Fig 3. This is a page from "P-46," one of the earliest codices of the NT that has survived. It is dated to about 200 CE, and contains significant parts of the "Pauline" Epistles. Notice that there are no spaces between words and no punctuation. Quite different from the clean and tidy form of the Bible we are treated to today—which comes complete with word separation, chapter divisions, punctuation, and even verse numbers! that the original author did not intend.

And permit me one final word on a biblical oddity relating to the language of Jesus. Most modern scholars believe that Jesus primarily spoke Aramaic. This is even indicated in several places in the New Testament (e.g., Matt. 27:46; Mk. 5:41). But the New Testament is written in Greek, not Aramaic, so ostensibly what we have in those writings are *Greek* translations of the *Aramaic* words of Jesus. Not an overly big deal, of course, but at least a significant one considering the relative importance of Jesus' words for the Christian faith. When you read an English Bible, you are thus reading *an English translation of a Greek translation of the Aramaic words of Jesus.*

So, to summarize, if you, as an average Christian, rely on the Bible as your transport into the supernatural world, keep this in mind: You are reading an anthology of books, internally inconsistent and in conflict with science, for which we have no original copies, composed in three different languages, and for which you must (unless you know Hebrew, Aramaic, and Greek) rely on an English (or other) language translation.

Doesn't really inspire much faith, does it?

So What CAN We Know about Supernatural Things?

I would conclude here by arguing this. The Biblical writings, interesting and academically valuable as they are, offer no truth whatsoever about the things we cannot see, hear, or feel. They are, like other religious documents produced over the course of history, merely the creations of men who claimed exclusive knowledge of things divine. In like fashion, Christian institutions or clerics have absolutely no knowledge whatsoever about what (if anything) lies behind the veil of our physical world. Therefore, I submit that Christianity—in ANY form—is of no value to anyone when it comes to informing us about the supernatural—and it may be that there is no "supernatural" at all. Stated another way, if you identify as a

Christian, you must 1) believe in the divinity of a book that contradicts both itself and science, and/or 2) believe in the teachings of a specific church (and there are hundreds of different ones that have contradictory teachings). Put simply, to do so just isn't rational.[1]

My first solid realization of this came in the form of this thought: "If I can't believe in Genesis 1 (and I certainly cannot), then I can't believe in John 3:16 either (the central teaching of much of Christianity). It is completely irrational to say that "some" parts of the Bible are divinely inspired (and thus true and historically correct) and some are not. *It all stands or falls together.*

So let me summarize the true state of our knowledge about supernatural or metaphysical things with a very simple illustration. Suppose you are walking down the hall in your home and notice that the door to the bathroom is closed. This seems odd to you, since both of your very young children are standing there and your wife is at work. You ask them why the bathroom door is closed, and (as precious children will often do) they give you two very imaginative answers. Your son gleefully declares, "Because there's an airplane in there!" You respond, "Oh I see! What kind of airplane?," and he says "A Boeing 747!!" At that moment your daughter objects and blurts out "No Daddy, he's wrong. There's a dinosaur in there!" Again, you smile and ask "What kind of dinosaur?," and she says "A T-Rex!!" Now, you KNOW, based on the very small dimensions of that bathroom, that neither of these very creative answers can be true. You just can't fit a Boeing jumbo jet or (even a baby) Tyrannosaurus Rex into such a small space. So your state of knowledge about what is really behind that door in that small bathroom space is as follows:

1) There is no Boeing 747 in there.
2) There is no T-Rex in there.
3) You don't know what or who-- *if anything or anybody*—is in there.

And so it is with our state of knowledge about what lies behind the veil of our physical world. Neither of the two main witnesses about the supernatural in Christianity (i.e., The Bible and The Church) are credible when they declare what is there. And they declare a *lot*. And the same can be said for any religion or philosophical system, since their *modus operandi* are essentially the same—relying on the alleged statements of "holy" men/women or on "holy" books.

In short, I can't declare what I DO believe about such matters (i.e., I'm still waiting on a credible witness to enlighten me), but I can certainly say what I DO NOT believe (e.g., any currently existing religious dogma at all).

But do not be discouraged or demoralized by this truth. I will, in the next chapter, suggest why life without Christianity (or any religion) can be a wonderful thing, and why real, positive, and meaningful living is not only possible, but very attainable, once you shed the oppressive chains of religious dogma.

ENDNOTES

1) For the sake of completeness, I should mention one other significant attempt at preserving Christianity in a post-enlightenment world—that of "Neo-Orthodoxy." Neo-Orthodoxy, or "New Orthodoxy," was an early 20th Century response to the failure of Protestant liberalism's "flowery" approach to the human condition which was demolished by the horror of World War 1. The premier names associated with the birth of this kind of Christianity were Karl Barth, Emil Brunner, and Paul Tillich. Neo-orthodoxy, while complex in its approach, generally regards Jesus—more so than The Bible— as "the Word of God." The Bible can "become" the Word of God in our experience insofar as it

points us to the real Word—-Jesus. Thus, the Bible can be historically inaccurate (and neo-orthodoxy accepts this fact) and still be a divine vehicle.

While it may have had noble intentions—i.e., to provide a more modern and intellectually acceptable way of experiencing Christianity—it is complete nonsense. It is essentially Christian "existentialism" and is again based on some presumption that the Bible provides generally accurate statements about Jesus and God. It does not, and therefore neo-orthodoxy is just another, more sophisticated, attempt to make Christianity palatable to the masses.

Chapter Eight
A BETTER WAY

(Freedom, Life, and Love)

There is no greater liberating force in life than the truth. Truth can move entire generations to behave in better ways, it can bring down the most odious of tyrants, it can heal the most broken of relationships, and from the shackles of oppressive religious thought it can liberate the soul into a lush garden of positive living.

There are two main ways that extracting oneself from the terrible yoke of Christian dogma—or for that matter religious dogma of any sort—can provide us with a better life. The first has to do with putting away long-held traditions about the subjects listed in the title of this book, and the second has to do with adopting a new and positive way of thinking about one's place in this grand scheme of existence we call "life."

LIBERATION FROM THE NEGATIVE IN CHRISTIANITY

I trust that the preceding chapters in this book have convinced the reader that the two main "witnesses" to the "truth" of Christianity have been shown to be completely unreliable, and in fact to be unworthy of anyone's trust to disclose anything whatsoever about a potential metaphysical world. The Bible is a collection of books, with contradictory and inconsistent messages, and the historical Church—whether Catholic or

Protestant—is equally inconsistent. No deity has spoken to mankind through either one of these alleged intermediaries, so we can safely say that the following conclusions naturally follow as a consequence of that truth.

1. HELL

There is no such place. It is an illusion, dreamt up by various peoples at various times in history, to either propagandize about their particular religious beliefs—i.e., "believe in our teachings or you'll suffer everlasting torment"—or in some cases perhaps to solve the uncomfortable ethical dilemma that "evil-doers" often enjoy prosperous and felicitous lives while here on earth. The latter is the "What about Hitler?" question—i.e., how could a man who inflicted such massive suffering on millions of people not get what is coming to him at some point? (He obviously didn't suffer much while he was alive). The answer, for those who argue this, is that he "got his" when he died (i.e., he went to Hell; or will go there after some supposed "Final Judgment") and will continue to "get his" throughout eternity.

But the actual truth is that there is absolutely no empirical evidence that such a place of retribution exists, and it seems that evil and megalomaniacal men often "get away with it" during their lifetimes. Of course, a great many despots, and evil persons of all sorts, suffer some retribution or come to a violent end because of their bad behaviors in this life. As examples, consider the infelicitous end of such monsters as Mussolini, Saddam Hussein, Gadhafi, and even Hitler himself.

So what does this mean for you and me? It simply means that you do not have to worry about ending up in such a horrible, barbaric, never-ending torture chamber when you die. If you've ever experienced any anxiety, large or small, about such a fate for yourself, STOP IT NOW! I can't tell you what, if anything, happens to our conscious selves at death, but I can categorically state that no eternal flame awaits you—no Christian Hell, Islamic Hell, Hindu Hell, or any currently proposed Hell whatsoever.

And if you still have a general fear of death, think of this fact. If we are simply biological beings, and we exist for but a brief moment in time, then *nothing* will happen at death. You will simply revert to your "non-existent state", and be as you were (so to speak) before you were born. Did you experience any fear, anxiety, pain, or discomfort at all before you took up residence in your mother's womb? Of course you didn't. And if this is all there is, you won't experience any after you die. To illustrate from my personal experience, I was born in 1952, and frankly I don't remember 1951 at all—or any year prior to it. That's because I "wasn't" prior to my birth.

Furthermore, as I heard Christopher Hitchens remark on more than one occasion, if this is "it" for us, you won't KNOW that you're dead after you die. So relax, the only real Hell you can ever experience is the one imposed upon you in this life by false religious dogma. Don't let it be so.

2. THE DEVIL AND DEMONS

There are no such beings. As we saw in earlier chapters, the idea of a personal devil was introduced into Jewish thought during the "intertestamental" period—the period between the writing of most of the Old Testament books and the writings included in the New Testament. The notion of demons was also a late development in historical thought. The inhabitants of Palestine in Jesus' day perceived of demons as evil beings which inhabited the bodies of humans, thereby causing all kinds of physical and mental illnesses. But of course we know today that neither sickness nor mental illness is caused by supernatural beings, but rather by the natural frailties of the human body and mind.

So what does this mean for you and me? It means that we don't have to fear a non-existent being or his supposed cohorts. They aren't there. Just as the very ancients mistakenly believed in a sort of animism—-that spirits or deities resided in rocks and trees, for example—-we are mistaken if we accept this nonsense. To again reference my personal experience, I used to occasionally wake up in the middle of the night and feel an evil "presence" in the room. It was often after having a dream in which Satan was chasing me, and I was holding a cross in my hand for protection. It's funny, but when I discovered that the whole Satan/Demons thing was fictional, the dreams and scary middle of the night experiences began to go away. And today, they are a distant memory.

So if you have anxieties about such things, fear not. Lucifer and his alleged posse are merely twisted concepts birthed by the ancient mind, and they do not exist.

3. SIN

There is no such thing. This concept is so much an ingrained part of our culture in America, that to question its existence seems absurd to many people. But as we saw in the earlier chapters, the concept of sin requires the existence of a specific God with a specific list of "no-no's." For sin to occur, it requires that a human being commit one of the acts on the no-no's list. But there is no Hebrew tribal god named Yahweh, who has a son named Jesus, and the alleged lists are creations from the minds of both the ancient Hebrews and New Testament writers.

Is there such a thing as "bad (or evil) behavior?" Of course there is, but such behavior is not an offense against any deity, and the listed Christian sins are not sins at all. For example, "adultery" is not a sin, but it can in many instances be bad behavior. I'll discuss this in greater detail shortly, but my point is that it is bad behavior because it often hurts people—a husband or wife, their children, or other relevant persons. The same can be said for so-called fornication, jealousy, anger, coveting, gossiping, etc., etc. In the case of fornication—-sex outside of marriage—I suggest that while it is not "sinful," it can occasionally be harmful to another person. One such example would be the case of the stereo-typical "ladies' man," who goes about seeking targets for sexual conquest, and lies them into bed. If you feign interest in a woman just to have sex with her—that is bad behavior. It eventually hurts her feelings, and that is selfish and unfair.

But consensual sex between two unmarried persons is not sin *or* bad behavior. It is as normal as breathing. And while we're on the subject of sex, let's not forget our homosexual human neighbors. Homosexuality is not sin, for the same reason given above—there's no such thing as sin. It is also not bad behavior, because science has recently shown us that a person's sexual identity has almost always been determined at birth.[1] Sexual preference usually is determined *for* you —and is not determined because you decide to have one inclination or another. I did not choose to be heterosexual, nor did most homosexuals choose to be gay. And even if there are examples where it is a choice, it is still not sin.

To be inclusive, we must also mention masturbation and "lust" in our discussion of sex. Both of these things are also as natural as breathing, and no one should feel otherwise. Nothing related to sex is a "sin," it is simply the way evolution has naturally wired us. Of course, like everything else we engage in, it should not be used in ways that are validly harmful to others or ourselves.

So what does this mean for you and me? It means we can now experience the liberating truth that you were not "born in sin, with a naturally evil heart," as Christian dogma would have you believe. Your choices for behavior are just that—-choices, and not sin. Of course, if you choose to behave badly—selfishly, deceitfully, unempathetically, violently, etc. —that's on you. You will experience the negative blowback of your behavior in the form of retaliation from other people or the law, and unless you're a sociopath you will also suffer pangs of conscience.

For years I believed the nonsensical Christian dogma that I was inherently evil, and that certain of my natural behaviors and inclinations were sin. But no more. I am a biological child of this planet, with my mammalian cousins, and there is nothing inherently bad about me. Or about you. I can, and do, choose to be empathetic and compassionate in my relationships with others, though granted I am not always 100% successful in my attempts. But that is always my goal.

4. The ANTICHRIST AND ARMAGEDDON.

These two things have to do with the future according to Christian dogma, and like the other things we have been discussing, *they do not (and will not) exist.* There is no coming anti-Christ who will "take over the world for a time," nor is there any coming divine, cosmic battle in which God will destroy his then current enemies. So stop looking for them. You can twist the numbers "666" all you want, and identify current nations with certain ancient biblical names or "prophecies," but these two ridiculous notions are a complete illusion. I have actually heard people in my community refer to our current President—Barack Obama—as the anti-Christ. I have also heard Christian preachers hold forth about Russia being one of the predicted nations who will come against Israel at the Battle of Armageddon. And throughout history, some Christians have identified all kinds of people and nations as the prophesied players in the final cosmic drama. But it's all nonsense. And highly destructive nonsense, at that.

So what does this mean for you and me? It means that we can stop believing this idiocy about mankind being in "the last times," and that the end of the world is just around the corner. The only way that the end of the world is just around the corner, is 1) if religious radicals or political extremists pursue the destruction that comes with an endless warring against each other (I'm thinking nuclear, biological, or chemical here), or 2) some random cosmic accident wipes us out (a huge asteroid strikes earth, a massive solar flare, a new disease epidemic, etc.), or 3) we ignore the wisdom of taking care of the planet, which feeds us and provides for all of our other needs.

But at least for the foreseeable future none of these things are likely to occur. So enjoy the longevity that you are granted. And most certainly do not fear some immanent Armageddon. There's no such thing.

LIBERATION INTO A POSITIVE, MEANINGFUL LIFE

I realize that my readers here may respond to what I've written in a variety of ways. If you are already an atheist or an agnostic, you may consider my argument in this book as merely "preaching to the choir." That is, Christianity does not affect you personally in one way or the other, because you already don't believe in it. Those who are "nominal" or even liberal Christians also likely suffer no pangs from the negativity of Christian dogma because they see nothing real or immanent about its more negative aspects. This may also be true for a great many conservative Christians, because they haven't thought with any depth about the serious ramifications of the very doctrines they say they believe. They truly don't consider the negative aspects of what they believe, and in fact whisk through life with the certitude that they will inherit Heaven and that God is personally focused on their well-being.

But for those who, like me, took all of the doctrines of Christianity seriously and pondered over the implications of each of them, I have some great news! The mental and emotional liberation you will experience when you once and for all acknowledge that they are merely illusions (and thus let go of them) is astounding! And this liberation is life-changing and life-affirming to a degree I can barely express! It could be likened, I suppose, to what a person feels like when he or she finally pokes their head above water after nearly drowning. It's a feeling of freedom, of an excessive weight being removed from your shoulders, and it is no less than earth-shattering!! Life can be tough enough without being saddled with the belief that people (or you yourself) are going to Hell, that you are a filthy sinner, that devils and demons are chasing you, or that we're staring at the end of the world.

When I first experienced that epiphany after years of evolving towards it, I cannot tell you how great it felt. I wanted to get up, go outside, and just sing and shout like I might have as a new Christian convert! (Ironic, huh?). It was the beginning of a new life for me—a life governed by the positive, by a full appreciation of all things that I was only able to partially value previously, and frankly by a new-found sense of my own worth that was often absent before. Suddenly it occurred to me that I was in control of most of my life, and that no other outside spiritual or metaphysical influences were involved.

And let me say that it takes a certain amount of courage and honesty to make the break, because you are going against the beliefs of the majority of society which at least nominally has faith in such things. And you are going against a belief system that you yourself have probably carried around for some number of years. But take heart in the fact that there is an ever-increasing number of us, and I imagine that in a decade from now those numbers will be significant. Probably not a majority number, but a significant one.

Let me also say that it doesn't take any courage at all to believe in Christianity, or in any such system of dogma. At least not in this country. It's easy to embrace a religious system which teaches that God is benevolently following you around at each moment of the day or night, and that in the end he has a big mansion awaiting you for eternity. What's hard about that? Nothing. The problem is, it's not true.

OK. So now that we have established that all Christian dogma that you may have picked up at various stages in your life is utterly *false*—and that you needn't be afraid of or controlled by it—where do you go from here? I would never presume to tell anyone exactly how they should readjust their perception of life, but I can offer some suggestions.

The first is to readjust your thinking about the value of *this* life, the "here and now". There is no credible evidence that we will experience any other conscious life except the one we have now, so *live as if this is it*. I have known more than a handful of people who believe that their suffering in life is brought on by God, and that this is a good thing. They believe that the more they suffer in the here and now, the more reward they will receive in Heaven after they die. Or they believe that God is "trying" them so that they will be better people. This is nonsense, and an evil of the highest kind. If you are suffering for any reason whatsoever, try and determine the actual real-time earthly cause of it, and then do something about it. You're not going to be awarded "brownie" points by some deity for enduring pain in this life. It might be that this life is the only one you'll have, so address the problem here and now. Here are some examples of our common human suffering for your consideration, and a few thoughts about how to address it:

In a bad marriage? Do *all that you can* to resolve the conflicts in it, but if after serious reflection over time you honestly determine that it can structurally never get better, then get out of it! If children are involved, go a thousand extra miles to assure them that your divorce has nothing to do with them, and make sure you love them with extra fervor so that they will have the best chance to develop as secure and happy individuals. Of course, divorce has consequences, but exposing a child to a hostile emotional environment for roughly two decades is worse than the alternative. Again, do everything in your power to repair the marriage and improve the communication with your spouse. But if that's not possible, then divorce can be the "lesser of two evils."

Have emotional problems? Do a little self-reflection and try to determine what they are. If you have trouble getting a grip on what's going on with your problems, go see a shrink or therapist who can help you sort out these kinds of things. (Of course, try and find a good one, because—like lawyers--there are a lot of bad ones out there).

Hate your job? Don't feel like the Lone Ranger, cause lots of Americans do. But instead of developing a martyr complex, try and examine ways to make your job more interesting or rewarding to you. Make an attempt to resolve any conflictual situations, and communicate with those whom you trust. But if you exhaust every possibility on that front and see no possible light at the end of the tunnel, then start looking for another one. (But carefully, please. The quality of the job market in this country is not what it used to be).

Lonely? Who isn't at one time or another? Get out there and find some friends. Or a partner. Remember, in the words of the Beatles, " ….in the end, the love you take, is equal to the love you make."[2] As with every other aspect of life, use wisdom when choosing friends or lovers. But take the proactive route, because if you do nothing, nothing is likely to happen. There is no evidence that a deity is behind the scenes plotting to drop a friend, or Mr./Ms. Right on you at just the right time.

Depressed? Again, most folks are at one time or another. Try and determine if your depression is caused by personal forces (bad job, strained personal relationships, lack of money for basic necessities, etc.), or if your depression may have a physical cause. Physical causes can be external (poor diet, lack of exercise or sleep, meds, etc.), or they can be internal (chemical imbalances in the brain, etc.). If the cause is personal, try and figure out a way to fix it. If it is physical, or simply too overwhelming for you to handle alone, go see a professional. There is NO shame whatsoever in seeking a therapist or a shrink. In fact, as I see it, our society would be in a lot better shape as a whole if a much larger segment of folks would do just that. Anybody who says that they wouldn't benefit from talking to someone who could help them sort out their emotional or psychological issues is not living in reality.

Hurting? If it's physical, go see a sawbones. It's about to become easier for many in this country to afford a trip to the doctor (due to healthcare reform legislation), so just do it. If it's emotional, try and understand that your pain has been shared by almost every other human being on this planet at one time or another. If the source of it is a partner who has rejected you, try and realize that that person would never have made you happy, because they were not fundamentally well suited to you. Or perhaps they never valued you properly. Or maybe he or she was just an asshole.

If you're hurting because someone you loved has died, remember that death is the ultimate common lot of us all. "Ain't nobody gettin' outta here alive!" a Wild West gunslinger once warned, and he was right on an existential level. And there is nothing you or I can do about that. You have to pay (death), if you are going to play (life). But keep in mind, the time that you had with that person, however long or short, has made your life richer and created a set of memories within you that no one can ever take away. They loved you while they were here, and that in itself is a cause for celebration. A mother, a father, a spouse, a friend, a relative, a hero—it matters not. These are the wonderful interpersonal designs that life has given us.

At 61 years of age and counting, I have experienced the loss of many people, and the hurt I've experienced has been very significant with each one. But I can say two things about the pain caused by death. First, time became a great mitigator of the pain. The passage of time will reduce your pain, and allow you to experience life's joy again. And second, once I adjusted my attitude about this terrible reality, the pain was again diminished to a degree. My attitude adjustment amounted to simply accepting that this is the way it is, I am not alone in it, and the love of family and friends was available to help me through it.

If you'll indulge me for a moment, I'd like to speak of a particular time when a great loss was softened by a family member. It happened when I lost my mother, with whom I was very close, about 4 years ago. Several months after she passed I went with my sister, her husband, and my niece to her graveside on a holiday. Nothing much was said during our walk to the gravesite, and I knew my sister, her husband, and my niece were experiencing their own grief as we stood beside the headstone. I was pretty emotional and therefore oblivious to my surroundings, but as we turned to walk back to the car something happened which might've seemed trivial to any bystander. My niece must've noticed the tears in my eyes and perceived my pain as I stood at the grave, because without speaking a word she came over and put her arm around me as we walked. Up to that point I had not been able to spend a lot of time with her, because she was working and was busy raising a pretty large family. Plus my own work schedule was also hectic. But at that moment I felt a sense of relief and peace because of her simple kind and loving squeeze, and I will never forget it.

My point here is that life can be a truly great and positive experience, if we'll just readjust our attitudes about it. Once you shed the oppressive chains of Christianity, or of any religion, you are truly free to reconstruct your overall life view, and to do so in a positive way. Indulge me one last time, and let me share how I reconstructed mine and deprogrammed myself in the process.

In the last 15 years I have begun to look at life as a wondrous thing. I mean, think about it. Here we are, on a tiny ball of dirt spinning through space and positioned at the outer edges of the massive Milky Way galaxy, and we are thinking, feeling, and living beings on it. The universe is so huge it's virtually impossible to fathom it all, yet here in our tiny corner we have all *this*. And what constitutes all "this?" Love, for example. Love for a child, a parent, a sibling, a lover, a friend, a pet, etc. Love is an amazing thing, even if it is a function of chemical activity in our brains. Art is another amazing thing, and takes many forms—-music, painting, sculpture, poetry, prose, etc. And don't forget about nature's beauty—the late evening landscape as the sun disappears behind the horizon, a clearwater bay in some part of the world (my favorite is Montego Bay in Jamaica), a Bluebird perched on a branch, stars in the clear night sky, space photographs of the earth and other planets, a Super Nova, a dolphin or a whale, just about any pet, and many other such things. And then there is the beauty associated with aspects of human behavior—a young child tightly clutching her mother's hand as they navigate the aisles in a retail store, a child's smile or laugh, the joy in a person's face when they re-encounter a loved one who has been away for a while, one person offering food to another who has been chronically hungry, the joy of a parent whose child has emerged after a successful surgical operation, sincere hugs between family members or friends, the joy of an artist whose work has been positively acknowledged by an appreciative public, the joy of a man or woman who for the first time discovers that their affection for another is shared, the pride of a parent at their child's school graduation, the beauty of a valid charitable organization dropping food or medical supplies off to persons who have no natural access to them, and many, many other similar things.

Now I am acutely aware that we in this country are the luckiest of all persons to be able to experience many of these things. Through no nobility of our own, we were randomly born in a land where the potential for a relatively high lifestyle is possible. There are millions of people in the world who routinely experience the ravages of hunger, disease, and oppressive social and political forces. There is death, sickness, misery, and the general malaise caused by poverty in many areas of the globe. Of course, we have some of that in our country, also, and it is experienced disproportionately among minorities and the poor. But relative to much of the world we generally have it pretty good. And as Americans most of us can enjoy those sunsets, those childrens' glances, nature's beauty, etc. because we're not starving to death or wondering where we're going to sleep that night. And as contentious as our politics can be, our fundamental political structure is strong and not subject to the same kind of instability inherent in many of the world's governments.

But to appreciate the best things in life, you must have an attitude that facilitates it. If you value the vanities of life—lots of money, status, massive amounts of possessions, and the like—then you will be less likely to appreciate the truly good things. Life and circumstance can turn the wealthy man or woman into a poor one in the blink of an eye, but nothing can separate us from the love of our children, parents, or friends. Now understand that I am not advocating the pursuit of poverty, or that "things" have no legitimate place in our experience. There is absolutely nothing wrong with pursuing wealth or comfort. Relative wealth can provide certain freedoms for us, and it can provide means whereby we can help family, friends, and the needy. But the *pursuit* of wealth should never become the *love* of wealth, because it's a *thing*. It's a thing that has no intrinsic value, as it consists of physical assets or numerical data logged into a database at a bank. And you sure as heck aren't going to take it with you when you die. No, having massive wealth says nothing about your value as a person.

The same is true with social status. If you get right down to the nitty gritty of it, social status is merely the perceptions that other human beings have of us inside their heads—a chemical reaction, if you will. There is no inherent value in that, even though it can feed our ego. Of course we all need the affirmation of others, but that is different from a need to be on the social pages of our local newspaper.

A BRIEF WORD ON "MAGICAL THINKING"

Believing in Christianity, or in any religious dogma, is a part of what can be defined as "magical thinking." I am not talking about the term as defined by clinical psychology, which refers to a specific mental disorder, but rather (as Wikipedia puts it) "the identification of causal relationships between actions and events where scientific consensus says that there are none." And we all have done that at some point in life.

For example, many of us have an irrational fear of the numbers "13" or "666," we feel uncomfortable if a black cat crosses our direct path, we avoid walking under a ladder, we fear breaking a mirror, and many such things. On the flip side we think that things like carrying a rabbit's foot, crossing our fingers, or using our birth date numbers on a lotto ticket can bring us good luck. That any of these things have an inherent ability to bring fortune or calamity has the backing of NO empirical evidence, and in fact are part of a way of thinking that reflects our need to stack the odds in our favor in a world that can at times be very cruel and ugly. There is certainly no shame in our wish to improve our lot in life, but the tools of superstition are not going to get the job done.

And Christianity, or any form of metaphysical belief system, is magical thinking on a grand scale. It inserts unseen forces into our perception of life to account for our various situations in life. But part of growing as a person—and adopting a more reality-based framework for our perception of life—is shedding this kind of thinking. The truth is that you didn't lose your job because a black cat walked across your path, your girlfriend or boyfriend didn't break up with you because you accidentally elbowed a mirror and cracked it, things don't "come in threes," etc. etc. etc. You lost your job because of truly causal issues—-e.g., your company had to downsize, you were late 50% of the time, etc. And you lost your lover because he or she no longer felt the relationship was of value to them, or perhaps she or he was just a selfish and morally-challenged person. And if you see a black cat walk across your path, it only means one thing (as Groucho Marx once quipped)—"the animal is going somewhere." If you walk under a ladder, it cannot harm you—unless, of course, you bump into it and a can of paint perched atop its shelf drops on your head. Friday the 13th means nothing, except that once in a while our calendar numbering system requires that the 13th day be a Friday.

Deprogramming ourselves from this general way of perceiving life can take time, or— if you are fortunate—not so much time. For me, it took time. A long time. But getting to that point will allow you to look more realistically at life, adjust your expectations and your behaviors accordingly, and take more responsibility for your own current status in it. There are very real causal events in our lives, but none of them have to do with things like demons or gods. And the good news is that you have the power, within yourself, to make the best of your circumstances and change your future. You are valuable, infinitely valuable, as a member of humanity. And you can change your perceptions, expectations, emotional state, and economic state once you realize the truth that supernatural forces have nothing to do with the equation.

WHAT ABOUT MORALITY?

Alright, so when you've shed the negative, cancerous delusion of Christianity (or any other religion), what do you do about adopting a code of morality? After all, conservative Christians are always arguing that if you jettison the Ten Commandments—or the later Christian codes of morality— it encourages a free-for-all mentality for one's moral behavior. You can lie, cheat, steal, wound, kill, and behave any old way you wish, because there is no divine accountability or punishment to deter you. Christian apologists also argue that if there is no Christian morality, then there is no acceptable morality at all. All of this is complete nonsense.

First of all, the "morality" practiced by Christians is itself derived from a hodge-podge of commandments, exhortations, and social mores cooked up by *men*. We have proved to anyone with an open and rational mind that the Bible is not an authoritative message from any god, and yet Christian morality derives from that very human collection of books. Sort of, at least. In some Christian circles, they go even farther than proscriptions in the Bible and include dancing, men with long hair, women who dress with a minimum of clothing or in slacks, smoking, drinking, cursing, heavy metal music, etc. as examples of sin or immorality—even though none of these are directly spelled out as sin in the Bible. But whether it's something derived from a specific "thou shalt not" in the Bible, or one of the extra-biblical things just listed, IT ALL COMES FROM THE MINDS OF MEN. And specifically, men whose perception of morality was influenced by priestly religious codes or who were following the socially accepted mores of their day.

So any construction of morality that I might build has just as much validity as (and more than, I would suggest) any ancient one. And I have constructed just such a code. A very simple code, and one that is shared by many atheists and agnostics. It states simply that the essence of morality is to "do good, and do no harm." This is closely related to the "Golden Rule" (Lev. 19:18; Lk. 6:31) which Jesus mentioned, but which was around long before he was. And this code is motivated by human empathy—the ability to consider the status and feelings of your fellow human beings.

This code may manifest itself in different ways, given different circumstances. For example, if I see a homeless person on the street and they ask me for money, I may or may not give it to them. If they reek of alcohol, and I suspect that they need extra money just to buy more booze, I probably won't give it to them. If, however, another such person seems to be genuinely in trouble, without sufficient funds for food, I very likely will help them out.

Or take another hypothetical instance—that of lying. If my daughter has been dating someone who turns out to be a violent person or a dangerous stalker, I will not hesitate to lie to him about her whereabouts. "Sure," I might say if he calls, "she's taken a job in Alaska." This would be an option, of course, if I had previously told him to leave her alone or suffer my physical wrath—and he ignored the warning. Anne Frank lied to the Nazis about her concealment of Jews during the Second World War, and in these kinds of cases even lying becomes the moral thing to do. Of course, for me, telling the truth and being up front in my daily social interaction is the rule, and lying would be the very rare exception.

But in each and every case my goal and intent is to do good, and to do no harm. The religionist may well ask, "But how do you know what good is, if you don't have God telling you what it is?" Again, good is what accrues to the benefit of others as well as to myself, and it is based on empathy and compassion. And there is no empirical evidence whatsoever that any deity has spoken to mankind at any time about what should be deemed good, or about anything whatsoever for that matter. But I'm still listening, and should a deity choose to declare anything to me, or to mankind as a whole, I will be the first to acknowledge it and submit myself to it. But up to the present, the silence has been deafening. If there *is* a deity, whose consciousness is similar to ours and he/she/it can thus communicate to us in a form we can understand, then he/she/it has chosen not to do so. And we have no control over that.

Let me share another measuring stick I use to evaluate goodness in myself and in other people. It is the "selfishness quotient," and can be illustrated by imagining the top half of a circular clock. (Or by glancing at one if it's nearby). Draw a straight line between the "9" and the "3," and imagine the 9 as representing 100% selfishness and the 3 as 100% unselfishness. Now imagine a single hand of the clock as indicating where, between the 9 and the 3, the relative selfishness or unselfishness of a person is located. The "9 o'clock person" represents a completely selfish person, concerned ONLY with how any event in life can benefit him or her. This is the narcissist, the self-obsessed person who has no compassion for others. He or she initiates every move in life to obtain the best possible result for him or herself, and could care less about how it might affect others. The "3 o'clock person" is the exact opposite, with no concern whatsoever for his or her own wants and needs, and lives only to benefit others. This person is a doormat for others to trample on, and never exercises any self-concern. They probably have no self-esteem, and perceive little value in themselves.

But most people probably live somewhere in between the 10 and the 2, though I have met a few 9 o'clockers, and perhaps a handful of 3 o'clockers. And neither of these extremes is desirable. But there is a whole range of behavior located between the 10 and the 2 that reflects our degree of selfishness. I myself try to live somewhere between the 12 and the 2—or at least in some zone where I am not merely half-selfish and half-unselfish (12 o'clock)—i.e., where I am more unselfish than selfish. This description of a "moral clock" may seem a little clinical or mechanical, and I certainly don't "grade" myself or others on such a numerical basis, but it is a way to perceive of the concept visually. In reality, I try to exercise empathy in all aspects of my personal and business life, and make sure that I treat others as I would like to be treated. This, for me, is the essence of morality and goodness. There are no lists, or enumerated specifics for my morality. I just know. Evolution has equipped me with a capacity to be empathetic, and to perceive how my actions will affect others. And to the extent that I practice my empathy, I am being moral and "good."

MY OWN OVERALL PERCEPTION OF LIFE

I am an agnostic. I have thought deeply, studied intensely, and have come to this philosophical position after many, many years of reflection. I am not so much the type of agnostic who says "we *can't* know about God's existence, or of metaphysical things" due to our physical and intellectual limitations. I am more the sort who believes "we *don't* know." In other words, it seems to me that if there were a deity whose essence included a thinking component that is much like ours, then that deity could certainly communicate with us. But after honest examination of ALL religions, alleged human "near-death experiences," and the endless metaphysical pronouncements from all kinds of characters from human history, I have concluded that no deity has done so.

And I'm not so certain that we're even capable of asking the right question in this regard. Our brains, complex and powerful as they are, are actually quite small in size. Perhaps we are like the butterfly who quite certainly does not have the same level of rational powers as we do, and who most certainly has no knowledge of our human experience. A butterfly has never asked the question, "Is there a human?," because it does not have the intellectual or rational power to form the thought. And maybe that is how it is with us. The early Hebrews and the later Christians, along with their foreign neighbors, sort of created God in their image. He had human characteristics such as thought and communication ability, emotion (jealousy, anger, love, hate, impatience, etc.), and even in very early texts had a human-like physical form (e.g., Gen. 3:8-24). But could it be that there is no God with a human-like mind, and that our ability to conceive of such is completely off base? If there is such a "being"—and here again perhaps even the notion of a *being* is a false notion—perhaps we don't have the capacity to understand it. At any rate, no deity has spoken to us, and no religion can legitimately claim that he/she/it has.

Now, as an agnostic, I don't claim to know about any potential metaphysical realities whatsoever. I can, however, by my intellectual stance, retain a kind of hope that I will consciously survive my death, and that such a post-death experience will be a positive one. I cannot honestly state with those who have adopted pure atheism as their stance, that I KNOW this is *it* for us. There is no credible evidence of life after death, of course, and so my atheist friends would no doubt ridicule my hope of something for which there is no evidence. I understand this, and they would be right to so ridicule, but there is a great difference between *hope* and *belief*. I observe the world, ponder our vast universe (or multiverse?), and all of the very awe-inspiring elements within it—the joy of experiencing the love of another human being, the ability to create things from within my mind, the vastness of "space," black holes, the laws of nature, and many such things. This gives me a sense that I don't know all there is to know about the universe and our existence. I had no hand in my conscious arrival on this planet, and I will have no hand in it when I breathe my last. Maybe I will survive my physical death, and maybe I won't. I wish I knew, but I don't. But at least I can have hope—hope that I will continue in my consciousness, and that the experience will be pleasurable. I will, however, live my life as if this IS in fact all there is—sort of a reverse Pascal's Wager[3] —and whatever happens *happens*. I can't say for sure what will be, but I can say for sure what won't be (i.e., the horrible things in the title of this book).

SOME PARTING THOUGHTS

We have come to the end of my consideration of the harmful effects of Christianity's barbaric negative dogma, but I want to leave you with a recap of certain truths and related conclusions contained in our study:

You are a member of the human race, and therefore are infinitely valuable.

There is no god who is going to "get you" or judge you at the end of your life.

There is no Hell that awaits you.

You were not born "evil."

There is no such thing as "sin."

We are not in "the Last Days."

Satan, and demonic beings, do not exist.

Consequently:

Love yourself, and others.

Try to live empathetically.

Do your best to enjoy your time here and now on earth.

Try to tip the scales of your life towards the "unselfish" side.

Pursue what is noble and good.

Never disconnect yourself from hope.

Fear nothing that you find in any religion—it's *all* an illusion.

And finally, adopt a positive attitude about life. Sure, it's tough at times—*very* tough—and there is ugliness somewhere in the world at any second of the day. But steer your life and thoughts in an affirmative way. We have this "gift" of our existence, so do all that you can to make it meaningful and enjoyable. Invest yourself in it with all the fervor of an athlete in training. In the words of a TV commercial from my younger years: "Try it, you'll like it." It really can be a wonderful thing, regardless of your circumstance in life.

When people ask me if I think the glass is "half full or half empty," I just respond "Hell, I don't know. I'm just glad I have something to drink!"

Now if you'll further indulge me, I'd like to leave you with a suggestion based on words from a 60's Broadway play entitled *Mame*. The words are my modern expansion of those spoken by the main character, Auntie Mame:

"Life is a smorgasbord, but most of us poor bastards just stand around at the salad bar!" (She actually said "Life's a banquet and most poor suckers are starving to death!"—but I like my adaptation better).

And my suggestion to you, with all sincerity and love, is:

"STOP STANDING AROUND AT THE SALAD BAR!!!"

ENDNOTES

1) Although homosexual orientation may or may not have genetic origins, it most certainly is already determined at birth (cf. the various studies by the National Institute for Mathematical and Biological Synthesis = NIMBioS).
2) Lyrics from the song "The End," from the album *Abbey Road*.
3) Blaise Pascal, in *Pensees*. A simple statement of "the Wager" goes like this: We cannot reasonably know if God exists or not. However, life is a "wager' in which each person *must* come down on one side or the other. If you wager that God does *not* exist and lose (because he does), you lose much (in the afterlife). If, however, you wager that he *does* exist and lose (because he does not), then you lose very little (maybe a little earthly pleasure or opulence). The problems with this wager are multiple, and have been discussed and de-bunked by many.

GLOSSARY OF TERMS

(as used in this book)

Anglican – Having to do with the Anglican Church, a tradition within Christianity comprising the Church of England and churches which are historically tied to it or have similar beliefs, worship practices, and church structures. The hierarchical head of the church is The Archbishop of Canterbury, and it is heavy on liturgy and sacraments. Many consider it a mix of Protestantism and Roman Catholicism, though it possesses no formal ties to either.

Anthology -- An anthology is a collection of literary works chosen by a compiler, or compilers. The Bible is an anthology.

Apocalypse – "The Apocalypse" refers to the events of the end of the world, when God puts down his enemies and ushers in his eternal righteous kingdom. (It can also refer to a literary work describing such events).

Apocalyptic Literature – A type of religious prophetic literature that contains fantastical images and surrealistic characters. An apocalypse is a literary report of an amazing, often fearful, violent vision that reveals truths about past, present, and/or future times in highly symbolic and poetical terms. The writer may represent himself as being transported into a heavenly realm, or the vision may be unveiled—and even interpreted—by an angelic messenger. Apocalyptic exhortations are aimed at chastening and reforming their hearers with promises of rewards and punishment in the coming "end times." (*New World Encyclopedia*). There was a lot of apocalyptic literature floating around Palestine between about 200 BCE and 100 CE, but little of it made its way into The Bible. The most obvious examples are the Book of Daniel and The Book of Revelation.

Apostles – The word literally means "one who is sent forth," and thus means "messenger" or "envoy." In the New Testament, Jesus' original twelve disciples are called "Apostles," Paul calls himself and Barnabus one, and there are hints that others were so considered.

Aramaic – A northwest Semitic language in common day-to-day use by the Jews between the periods of about 539 BCE and 70 CE. It was most probably the main language of Jesus, and was the written language of a few parts of the Old Testament. Although it was a cousin of the Hebrew language, it was nonetheless very distinct.

Babylon -- One of the most powerful and famous cities (city-states) of ancient Mesopotamia. Situated about 55 miles south of modern-day Bagdad, Iraq, its armies subdued and carried into exile much of Judah in the 6th Century BCE.

BCE – "Before the Common Era." It is the equivalent of the older "B.C." (which meant "before Christ.")

Canaan – The geographical area which in ancient times was located from about where modern-day Syria is to the northeastern edge of modern Egypt. In other words, it occupied the location of modern Israel and large parts of the surrounding areas. Canaan had a history stretching back to long before the Hebrews took over the area, and "the Canaanites" were the native inhabitants of that land. It is not known whether the Israelites were a separate ethnic people who invaded Canaan from the outside (as the Bible says), or whether they were themselves a Canaanite tribe who eventually dominated other Canaanite tribes and took over the land.

Canon – "Collection" of books. An anthology. As it relates to both the Old and New Testaments, the "canon" of Scripture means the books accepted as "holy" or "authored by God" by Christians and Jews. Protestant and Catholic Christians accept a similar canon—although Catholics add the Apocrypha to the Protestant canon—while Jews only accept the Old Testament (and thus call it "The Hebrew Bible" or "The Tanach"—an acronym for "The Law, the Prophets, and The Writings").

Canonization – The act of declaring something to be "canonical," or "special." In the case of the biblical writings, they were declared "canonical" or "holy" by various groups long after they were written.

Catholic Church – The form of the Christian Church that traces its origin back to the Apostle Peter, the alleged first "Pope." The word "Catholic" means "universal."

CE – "Common Era." It is the equivalent of the older "A.D." ("Anno Domini," meaning "Year of Our Lord.")

Church – The institutional, organized church of any type. Churches usually have a unique hierarchy, and a formal statement of beliefs.

Cleric – A member of the clergy in any religion. A formal leader in a religious organization.

Composite Greek text – The Greek text of the New Testament which scholars speculate best matches the original New Testament writings.

This speculation is based upon comparing thousands of existing copies from many different dates and geographical locations. We don't actually know how closely they resemble the original separate writings, because we don't have the originals.

De facto – "in practice or actuality, but not officially established or ordained by law."

Dead Sea Scrolls -- A group of texts found between 1946 and 1956 near the Dead Sea, at Qumran. The texts date from the 2nd Century BCE to the 1st Century CE, and are made up of fragments of Old Testament manuscripts (ca. 40%), extra-canonical books from the Second Temple period (ca. 30%—e.g., The Book of Enoch, Wisdom of Sirach, etc.), and other writings which represent the religious views of some sectarian party within Judaism (30%—e.g., Community Rule, The War Scroll, etc.). Of particular interest to Old Testament textual critics is the near-complete scroll of Isaiah, which generally matches the much later copies of the book. This suggests that the Jews who copied the books over the centuries were very careful in their work. Not perfect, but careful.

Denominations – Recognized autonomous branches of Christianity. E.g., Methodists, Baptists, Lutherans, etc.

Doctrine – A body of ideas taught to people as truth or as being correct. Doctrinal Statements are documents which clearly state what each church denomination believes about various religious concepts.

Dogma – A synonym of the word "doctrine," but with a bit more emphasis. "Doctrine" is sort of a neutral term for religious teaching, while "dogma" emphasizes the authoritative nature of that teaching.

Deuteronomist – The author (or authors) of the "D" source material found in the Pentateuch, who also edited and compiled the final form of the books of Joshua, Judges, Samuel, and Kings.

Documentary Hypothesis – The theory that the Pentateuch (Genesis through Deuteronomy) was not composed as a continuous narrative by one person, but rather that it contains material from four (or more) sources that was redacted into a continuous narrative by a final editor. The four main sources assumed are "J" (Yahwist), "E" (Elohist), "P" (Priestly), and "D" (Deuteronomist). This would explain differences in viewpoint, historical details, god names, and style found in the Pentateuch. It well explains why parallel but contradictory narratives appear in the Pentateuch. This theory has undergone intense scrutiny and development over the last century and a half, but is still widely accepted by biblical scholars today.

E.g. – "For example"

Ebionites – One of the 3 main sects of early Christianity established immediately after Jesus' time. This group believed that Jesus was the awaited Jewish Messiah, but that he was not divine. They also believed that keeping the laws of Judaism was necessary, along with faith in Jesus, for a person to be saved.

Empirical -- Provable or verifiable by experience or experiment. Empirical evidence is based on fact, as opposed to theory or speculation.

Evangelical – A somewhat ambiguous term referring to that group of Christians who emphasize the necessity of a "born-again" conversion, a conservative (but not necessarily inerrant) view of the Bible, and the central importance of Jesus' crucifixion and resurrection. An evangelical

Christian can be a member of any Protestant denomination or in fact of the Catholic Church, or no church at all. (See "Fundamentalist").

Fundamentalist -- Another somewhat ambiguous term referring to that group of Christians who believe in the 5 "fundamentals" of the faith: the inerrancy of the Scriptures, the virgin birth and deity of Jesus, the doctrine of substitutionary atonement, the bodily resurrection of Jesus, and the bodily second coming of Jesus Christ. It is a slightly somewhat more narrow and conservative term than "evangelical," although there are more similarities than differences between the two. (See "Evangelical").

Gehenna – The term most frequently translated "hell" in modern translations of the New Testament. The word itself is a transliteration of the Hebrew words "gay-hinnom" ("The Valley of Hinnom"), which in the earliest days of the Hebrews referred to the Valley of Hinnom located at the base of Mt. Zion.

Hades – a place where both righteous and wicked people go after death, perhaps with a separate compartment for each. It differs from the term "Gehenna" in the New Testament, which seems to be exclusively the destination for the wicked.

Heresy -- Unorthodox religious opinion. An opinion or belief that contradicts established religious teaching, especially one that is officially condemned by a religious authority.

I.e. – "That is"

Indulgences – The temporary forgiveness or mitigation of sins in the practice of the Catholic Church. During the Reformation, these forgivenesses were being sold (for money) to church-goers, a fact which angered the Protestant reformers like Luther and Calvin.

Inerrant (Inerrancy) – "Without error." As used by Biblical literalists, the "inerrancy" of the Bible means that it is completely true and without error in all of its statements—whether statements about historical events (Creation, the Exodus, King David's exploits, Jesus' life and resurrection, Paul's travels, etc. etc.), or statements about "spiritual" realities (the God Yahweh, sin, demons, Satan, etc. etc.).

Inspiration – The inspiration of the Biblical writings, according to Christian doctrine, states that the authors were led or influenced by God with the result that their writings may be designated "The Word of God."

Irenaus – The Bishop of Lyons, born sometime between 115 and 142 CE, most notable for his writings against the Gnostics.

Intertestamental Period – The period, defined by Christians, between the writings of the Old Testament and the New. Lots of imaginative doctrine was born in this period (Hell, Satan, demons, etc.) which found its way into the New Testament.

Jan Hus – (1369-1415). The first known Church reformer, who lived before Calvin, Luther, and Zwingli. He was burned at the stake as a heretic by the Catholics.

John Wycliffe – (1330-1384). English theologian, philosopher, church reformer, and promoter of the first complete translation of the Bible into English. He was one of the forerunners of the Protestant Reformation.

John Calvin – (1509 – 1564). A prominent Christian theologian during the Protestant Reformation and the namesake of the system of Christian theology called "Calvinism." His main work, *"The Institutes of the Christian Religion,"* was the most highly developed systematic theology produced up to that time. He is perhaps best known for developing the doctrine of "predestination," which claims that only those whom God "elects" will become Christians. For Calvin, God was omnipotent—a strong Deity whose will controls all of life's events—and man is but a respondent in the Divine play.

Judaism - The religion, philosophy, and way of life of the Jewish people.

King Josiah – (649–609 BCE). A king of Judah (from 641–609 BCE), according to the Old Testament, who instituted major reforms. He is credited by most historians with having established or compiled important Hebrew Scriptures during the Deuteronomic reform that occurred under his rule.

Koine Greek – "Common" Greek. The street form of Greek used by much of the Middle East in Jesus' day. It was in this form of Greek that the New Testament documents were written.

Martin Luther – (1483–1546). The most influential Reformer of the Christian Church in the 16th Century. Luther was a German monk who struggled in his early life with a great fear of Hell. At some point he had an epiphany and believed that the Catholic Church was corrupt and full of false teaching. He particularly hated their selling of indulgences as a means to salvation and the notion that the Pope was infallible. Eventually, he published his "95 Theses" which attacked a great deal of Catholic Doctrine. Out of this widely published anti-Catholic doctrine the Protestant reformation was born. Its war cries were "Sola Scriptura" ("Scripture Only," as opposed to "Scripture and the Pronouncements of the Catholic Church"), and "Sola Fides" ("Faith Only," as opposed to "faith, good deeds, and observance of Catholic sacraments and rituals" as the necessary requirements for salvation).

Masoretes – (The "Tradition-Keepers"). Groups of Jewish scribe-scholars who worked between the 5th and 10th centuries CE, based primarily in what is present-day Israel in the cities of Tiberias and Jerusalem, as well as in Iraq (Babylonia). Each group compiled a system of pronunciation and grammatical guides in the form of diacritical notes on the external form of the Biblical text in an attempt to fix the pronunciation, paragraph and verse divisions, and cantillation of the Old Testament for the worldwide Jewish community. The most well-known family of Masoretes was that of Ben Asher.

Meme --An idea, behavior, or style that spreads from person to person within a culture. A meme acts as a unit for carrying cultural ideas, symbols, or practices that can be transmitted from one mind to another through writing, speech, gestures, rituals, or other imitable phenomena. Supporters of the concept regard memes as cultural analogues to genes in that they self-replicate, mutate, and respond to selective pressures. (Wikipedia)

Mesopotomia – (Literally "between rivers" in Greek). It refers to the land between the Tigris and Euphrates Rivers, occupied by various peoples throughout history, and considered by historians as the cradle of civilization. Ancient Mesopotamia was located roughly where modern Iraq (plus surrounding territory) is today.

Messiah – the Anointed One whom the ancient Hebrews believed was to come and save them from their many enemies. Christians believe that this Anointed One was Jesus of Nazareth, but that his salvation of Israel is yet to come. (Although some Christians believe that the Church is the "New Israel").

Metaphysical – As used in this book, it refers to anything that could be considered "supernatural"—God, the Devil, Demons, angels, Heaven,

Hell, etc. (Meta-physical literally translates as "beyond physical", meaning "beyond the material, physical world").

Nag Hammadi – A city in modern-day Egypt, where 13 "books" (and other fragments of books) were found in 1945. These works were mostly Gnostic in content, and date to early Christian days (2nd Century CE). The most famous one is probably The Gospel of Thomas.

Nero – The 5th Emperor of Rome (54-68 CE), stepson and heir of the Emperor Claudius. He was not a particularly nice or stable fellow, and is likely the "anti-christ" who is referred to in the Book of Revelation.

Original manuscript – An original writing by an author, as opposed to a copy.

Original Sin – The doctrine that Adam and Eve's sin in the Garden of Eden was committed by all humans also, who are their descendants. This original sin we supposedly all committed has left every one of us with a "sin nature," or an embedded character trait that makes us naturally predisposed to "sin."

Papacy -- The office of the Pope, or the succession of the line of Popes.

Papal Succession -- The Catholic doctrine that the line of Papal authority began with the Apostle Peter—the first Pope—and continues to the present day (in Pope Francis, as of this writing).

Pentateuch – ("Five Scrolls"). The first five books of the Bible, as organized by both Jews and Christians (= Genesis through Deuteronomy).

Pharisee – A member of one of the influential ancient Jewish religious group of Jesus' day. The Pharisees followed the Oral Law in addition to the Torah (the Pentateuch) and attempted to live in a constant state of purity. Jesus allegedly called them "Vipers" and other derogatory names.

Pontiff – The Pope.

Pontifical Biblical Commission -- An organism established in 1902 within the Catholic Church to ensure the proper interpretation and defense of Sacred Scripture.

Postmortem – "after death"

Prophets – The second of three major divisions of the Hebrew Bible (the Old Testament) by Judaism—the first being "The Law" and the third being "The Writings." The Prophets are further subdivided into "The Former Prophets" and "The Latter Prophets."

Protestant Church – The form of the church that split off from the Catholic Church in the 16th Century. They "protested" against Catholic doctrines and practices, such as Papal authority and the selling of indulgences as a means to salvation.

Proto-Orthodox – The group of early Christians—with particular doctrinal views and views about which circulating books were sacred—who eventually won out and established what is today orthodox Christianity. The other two main groups, declared to be heretics by the proto-orthodox group, were the Ebionites and the Gnostics.

Puritans -- A group of Protestants that arose in the 16th century within the Church of England, demanding the simplification of doctrine and worship, and greater strictness in religious discipline. The Puritans believed that the Anglicans (the Church of England) had not gone far enough in their reformation away from the Catholic Church, and thus established a very detailed code of personal behavior.

Radiometric dating -- A technique used to date materials such as rocks, usually based on a comparison between the observed abundance of a naturally occurring radioactive isotope and its decay products, using known decay rates. The use of radiometric dating was first published in 1907 by Bertram Boltwood. It is now the principal source of information about the absolute age of rocks and other geological features, including the age of the Earth itself, and can be used to date a wide range of natural and man-made materials. Together with stratigraphic principles, radiometric dating methods are used in geochronology to establish the geological time scale. Among the best-known techniques are radiocarbon dating, potassium-argon dating and uranium-lead dating. By allowing the establishment of geological timescales, it provides a significant source of information about the ages of fossils and the deduced rates of evolutionary change. Radiometric dating is also used to date archaeological materials, including ancient artifacts. (Wikipedia)

Reformation (Protestant) – The 16th Century schism within Christianity initiated by Luther and Calvin (and earlier by Hus and Wycliffe). They "protested" many things then current in the Catholic Church (selling of indulgences, Papal authority, works-based salvation, etc.), and their efforts led to a whole new worldwide division within Christianity (i.e., Protestantism). Their watch words were *Sola Scriptura* ("Scripture Only") and *Sola Fides* ("Faith Only").

Shades – Shadowy figures who inhabited "Sheol" in the Old Testament. They possessed neither personality nor strength, and were just sort of "there." All persons—whether righteous or wicked—were thought to become Shades in Sheol upon death in the mind of the ancient Hebrews.

Sheol – The abode of the dead in the Old Testament. A place of darkness, stillness, and separation from God, inhabited by the "shades" (i.e., shadowy figures comprised of all dead people, whether righteous or wicked). It apparently was thought to be located under the surface of the earth, but was not any sort of "Hell" or place of divine punishment.

Sola Scriptura – Latin for "Scripture Only."

Sola Fide – Latin for "Faith Only."

Sin Nature – The theological doctrine that all human beings have an intrinsic nature built into them at conception (or birth) that causes them to sin. This nature was allegedly acquired by the fact that all humans are descended from Adam, who himself acquired this nature when he sinned in the Garden of Eden (Gen. 3).

Tartaros – In Greek mythology, the pit far beneath Hades where the Titans were imprisoned. The word (in the form of a verb) is used only in 2 Pet. 2:4 in the New Testament, and refers to a dark place where sinning angels were cast and chained until judgment day.

Textual Criticism – The science of studying the vast amount of biblical manuscript copies in order to try to get back to the wording of the original documents (which we do not have).

Temple – The central place of worship in ancient Judaism. There were two main temples in historical times, both located where The Dome of the Rock sits today in Jerusalem. The first was allegedly constructed by King Solomon in the 10th Century BCE, and the second by the Jews returning home from Babylonian captivity in the 5th Century BCE. Both were destroyed, and many Jews and Christians believe that a third temple will be constructed on that site in the future.

Theology – The large body of literature that sprang up after the Bible became a distinct, identifiable "book." Its purpose was to explain—in a neat, organized way—the great mass of varying statements and concepts found in the Bible. Systematic theologies are organized by topics; e.g., "God," "Sin," "Holy Spirit," "Hell," etc.

Torah – The first five books of the Bible (Genesis through Deuteronomy). "Torah" literally means "teaching" or "law," and is the first of a tripartite division of the Old Testament according to Judaism. (The second and third are "The Prophets" and "The Writings").

Transmission – A word denoting the process of copying and disseminating the various original books of the Bible in the ancient world.

Trinity – The Christian doctrine that God is one being made up of three distinct persons—Father, Son, and Holy Spirit. It is not stated clearly anywhere in the Bible, but later theologians argued over the concept and established detailed doctrinal statements about its nature.

Ulrich Zwingli – (1484-1531). The most important leader of the Protestant Reformation in Switzerland. Unlike Luther and Calvin, he was the only Reformer whose views did not evolve into an organized church denomination.

Vowel Pointings – The diacritical markings added to the Hebrew Bible (Old Testament) beginning with the Masoretes in about the 7th Century CE. Since the written Hebrew of the Old Testament originally had no letters to indicate vowel sounds, the Masoretes invented some and added them to the consonantal text. They did this to facilitate the reading and chanting of the Old Testament in liturgical settings. It's important to understand that Hebrew—like all languages—has always had vowel *sounds*, but was written in ancient (and indeed modern) times without any symbols to indicate what they are. However, context usually makes clear what vowels are intended to be vocalized.

Writings – The third and final division of the Hebrew Bible (the Old Testament) according to Judaism. The first two are "The Law" and "The Prophets."

Yahweh – The name of the tribal god of the ancient Israelites and Judeans. The earliest forms of the name were written (as was all Hebrew literature) without vowels, so the actual pronunciation is uncertain. That is, the name was written consonantally as "YHWH" and could be vocalized in several different ways. However, there is pretty good evidence that the actual pronunciation was "Yahweh," which translates as "he causes to be" or "he creates." In later times, the name was regarded as too "holy" to be pronounced, so the Masoretes inserted the vowels for the word "Adonai" (meaning "Lord, master") in the name, indicating that "Adonai" was to be pronounced instead of "Yahweh." Most Christian Bibles thus translate "Yahweh" as "THE LORD" (with caps), following the lead of the Masoretic tradition. "THE LORD," however, is not a proper name like "Yahweh" is, and it may be that Christian tradition feels uncomfortable with being identified as "Yahwists" like the ancient Israelites and Judeans.

95 Theses – Martin Luther's treatise that he allegedly nailed to the front door of All Saints Church in Wittenberg, Saxony, in the Holy Roman Empire in 1517. These documents protested against what Luther saw as clerical abuses by the hierarchy of the Catholic Church—particularly the sale of indulgences. They are widely regarded as the catalyst for the Protestant Reformation.

FOR FURTHER READING

Barker, Dan. *Godless*: How an Evangelical Preacher Became One of America's Leading Atheists. Ulysses Press, 2008.

Barker. *Losing Faith in Faith*: From Preacher To Atheist. Freedom from Religion Foundation, Inc., 1992.

Bernstein, Alan E. *The Formation of Hell*: Death and Retribution in the Ancient and Early Christian Worlds. Cornell University Press, 1993.

Carrier, Richard. *Why I Am Not A Christian*: Four Conclusive Reasons To Reject The Faith. Philosophy Press, 2011.

Davis, Mike. *The Atheist's Introduction to the New Testament*: How the Bible Undermines the Basic Teachings of Christianity. Outskirts Press, Inc. 2008.

Dawkins, Richard. *The God Delusion*. Bantam Books, 2006.

Dawkins. *The Magic of Reality*: How We Know What's Really True. Free Press, 2011.

Ehrman, Bart D. *Jesus, Interrupted*: Revealing the Hidden Contradictions in the Bible (And Why We Don't Know About Them). HarperCollins, 2009.

Ehrman, *Misquoting Jesus*: The Story Behind Who Changed the Bible and Why. HarperCollins, 2005.

Helms, Randel McCraw. *The Bible Against Itself*: Why The Bible Seems To Contradict Itself. Millennium Press, 2006.

Hitchens, Christopher. *god is not Great*: How Religion Poisons Everything. Twelve Books, 2007.

Loftus, John, ed. *The Christian Delusion*: Why Faith Fails. Promethius Books, 2010.

Long, Jason. *Biblical Nonsense*: A Review of the Bible For Doubting Christians. iUniverse, 2005.

Price, Robert M. *The Case Against The Case for Christ*: A New Testament Scholar Refutes the Reverend Lee Strobel. American Atheist Press, 2010.

Shelley, Bruce L. *Church History in Plain Language*. Thomas Nelson, 2008.

Spong, John Shelby. *Rescuing the Bible from Fundamentalism*: A Bishop Rethinks the Meaning of Scripture. HarperCollins, 1991 (originally).

Spong, *Re-Claiming the Bible for a Non-Religious World.* HarperOne, 2011.

Turner, Alice K. *The History of Hell.* Harcourt, Inc., 1993

Tarico, Valerie. *The Dark Side*: How Evangelical Teachings Corrupt Love and Truth. Dea Press, 2006.

Wells, Steve. *The Skeptic's Annotated Bible.* SAB Books, 2013.

Winell, Marlene. *Leaving the Fold.* New Harbinger Publications, 1993.

www.ingramcontent.com/pod-product-compliance
Lightning Source LLC
Chambersburg PA
CBHW031418290426
44110CB00011B/440